ANCIENT-FUTURE
EVANGELISM

ANCIENT-FUTURE FAITH SERIES

ANCIENT-FUTURE
EVANGELISM

Making Your Church a Faith-Forming Community

ROBERT E. WEBBER

Baker Books

A Division of Baker Book House Co
Grand Rapids, Michigan 49516

© 2003 by Robert E. Webber

Published by Baker Books
a division of Baker Book House Company
P.O. Box 6287, Grand Rapids, MI 49516-6287
www.bakerbooks.com

Second printing, April 2004

Printed in the United States of America

Library of Congress Cataloging-in-Publication Data

Webber, Robert.
    Ancient-future evangelism : making your church a faith-forming community / Robert E. Webber.
        p.   cm. -- (Ancient-future faith series)
    Includes bibliographical references. (p.   ) and index.
    ISBN 0-8010-9160-8 (pbk.)
    1. Evangelistic work. 2. Spiritual formation. I. Title. II. Series.
BV3793.W38 2003
269'.2—dc22   2003015441

Appendix 4, "The Eastbourne Consultation Joint Statement on Discipleship," appears courtesy of Cook Communications Ministries. ©1997. Used by permission of Cook Communications Ministries, 4050 Lee Vance View, Colorado Springs, CO 80918. A ministry dedicated to the proclamation of the Gospel and the support of believers on their discipleship journey.

Unless otherwise indicated Scripture is taken from the HOLY BIBLE, NEW INTERNATIONAL VERSION®. NIV®. Copyright © 1973, 1978, 1984 by International Bible Society. Used by permission of Zondervan. All rights reserved.

Scripture marked NRSV is taken from the New Revised Standard Version of the Bible, copyright 1989 by the Division of Christian Education of the National Council of the Churches of Christ in the USA. Used by permission.

CONTENTS

TABLES

INTRODUCTION TO THE ANCIENT-FUTURE FAITH SERIES

In each book of the Ancient-Future Faith series I will present an issue related to faith and Christian practice from a particular point of view—that of drawing wisdom from the past and translating these insights into the present and future life of the church, its faith, worship, ministry, and spirituality. In these books I address current issues in the context of three very significant quests taking place in the church today.

First, these books speak to the longing to discover the roots of the faith in the biblical and classical tradition of the church. I affirm the Bible as the final authority in all matters of faith and practice. However, instead of disregarding the developments of faith in the church, I draw on the foundational interpretation of the church fathers and the creeds and practices of the ancient church. These are sources in which Christian truth has been summarized and articulated to expose and defend against heretical teaching.

Second, this series is committed to the current search for connection to history. Therefore, I draw from the entire history of the church together with its many manifestations—orthodox, Catholic, and Protestant—particularly the Reformers and evangelicals like John Wesley and Jonathan Edwards. Valuable insights from these traditions are woven into the text, so the reader will understand how deeply committed Christians from various traditions have sought to think and live the faith in other places and times. From them we gain great wisdom.

Finally, I regard these insights and practices from the biblical tradition, ancient roots, and Christian history to constitute the foundation for addressing the third issue faced by today's church: How do you deliver an authentic faith into the new cultural situation of the twenty-first century? How do you carry the great wisdom of the past into a postmodern and post-Christian world? The way into the future, I argue, is not innovation or a new start for the church. Rather, the road to the future runs through the past.

These three—roots, connection to history, and authenticity—will help us maintain continuity with historic Christianity as the church moves forward in a changing world. I hope what I cull from the past and then translate and adapt into the present will be of benefit to your ministry in a postmodern, post-Christian world.[1]

ACKNOWLEDGMENTS

No one is fully able to acknowledge all the sources and people who contribute to the writing of a book. Many unnamed books, people, and even institutions have formed my life and challenged me to be sensitive to the work of the church as it moves into a post-Christian world. The fact that I mention only a few of these people and institutions here in no way diminishes my appreciation for the unnamed.

First, I need to thank Northern Seminary for my appointment as the William and Geraldine Myers Professor of Ministry. This generous chair has substantially reduced my teaching load, allowing me more time to write. I am equally grateful to Baker Books and especially to Robert Hosack for the support given to this series and for the freedom they have given me to develop this book in a way that reflects my convictions.

Next, there are those special people who have encouraged me and helped me with research and the process of many rewrites and editorial changes. A special word of thanks to Lois Stück and Chad Allen for their careful editing. Thanks to Ashley Olsen and Barbara Wixon at Northern Seminary for their cheerful and willing help. Also to Carmen Martinez, my ready and helpful assistant at the Institute for Worship Studies. Finally, and certainly not the least, I owe a debt of gratitude to my wife, Joanne. The freedom she gives me to spend long hours at writing and editing is a gift without which this book would be no more than unfinished thoughts.

INTRODUCTION

In September 1999, 450 church leaders from fifty-four countries and nearly ninety Christian fellowships and denominations met in Eastbourne, England, for the International Consultation on Discipleship to discuss a burning issue. The question they addressed is one that every pastor and congregation in the world has faced. How can our evangelism produce not only converts but disciples who grow in faith and become active members of the church?

In a published document entitled "The International Consultation on Discipleship," the authors acknowledged:

- "Many converts to Christianity throughout the world fall away from faith."
- The church is "marked by a paradox of growth without depth."
- "Many within the church are not living lives of biblical purity, integrity and holiness."[1]

In addressing the participants of the International Consultation on Discipleship, John Stott said that evangelicals have "experienced enormous statistical growth . . . without corresponding growth in discipleship."[2] African theologian Tokunboh Adeyemo lamented that the church "is one mile long, but only one inch deep."[3]

So, what are Christian leaders to do? To begin, declares the conference manifesto, the Great Commission is not only to evangelize but to *make disciples*. The document defines discipleship as "a process that takes place within accountable relationships over a period of time for the purpose of bringing believers to spiritual maturity in Christ."[4]

Note three very crucial insights for evangelism that result in discipleship:

- Evangelism is a process.
- Evangelism takes place over a period of time.
- Evangelism brings new believers to spiritual maturity.

13

To accomplish these goals, the conferees called Christians to recover the integral relationship between evangelism and discipleship, to assess rigorously existing structures, to recognize the local church as the primary community in which discipleship takes place, to affirm the vital role of mentoring, to rediscover the role of the Holy Spirit as teacher, and to call all Christians to live as "subjects in the kingdom of God."[5]

David Neff, an editor of *Christianity Today*, commented on the International Consultation. "Now that the consultation has placed disciple-making higher on the global evangelical agenda, it is vital that our biblical scholars, theologians, and spiritual guides develop for us a full-orbed vision of the life of the disciple."[6] *Ancient-Future Evangelism* is a response to this challenge. I come to this question, not out of my own imagination or ingenuity, but from an approach to evangelism, discipleship, and Christian formation rooted in Scripture, attested to in the history of the church, and authentic to the post-Christian world in which we live.

In chapter 1, I provide a survey of how Christians have been evangelized and formed as disciples throughout the centuries. This overview leads the reader directly to part 1, "The Process of Christian Formation," in which I present the process of the faith-forming church by discussing the four stages of growth and spiritual maturation developed by the ancient church.

Chapter 2 looks specifically at the development of the process of Christian formation in the ancient church. In chapters 3 through 6, I translate the ancient process into the task of making disciples in our post-Christian world.

In chapter 3, I show how the church may evangelize in today's world, commenting on how evangelism occurs by way of a community that lives out the message. In this way, involvement with the church is the context in which the seeker first experiences the message as a lived reality. Then, in the worship of the church, the message of Jesus is preached and enacted. Evangelism occurs as the seeker surrenders to Jesus Christ as personal Lord and Savior. Faith is formed in the church and through its worship. Initial Christian formation has begun. A passage rite transfers the new convert into the next stage.

The second stage of faith formation is initial discipleship (chapter 4). Through discipleship the new believer is brought into a deeper knowledge of his or her relationship with Jesus Christ. In this stage the new believer learns more about what it means to be a part of the church and a worshiper. The new convert is taught disciplines of the Spirit that bring depth to his or her spiritual commitment. Another passage rite moves the new disciple into the next stage.

In the third stage of faith formation, the new convert is introduced to the spiritual life (chapter 5). New Christians are taught that spirituality is a gift. Baptism is the image of the gift. Having been baptized into his death, Christians are called to die to sin. Having been baptized into his resurrection, Christians are called to live the new life in Christ by the Spirit. In this stage new Christians are taught how their own struggle to live the Christian life is a microcosm of the great battle with evil and how Jesus, who is the Victor over sin and death, is the one who by the power of the Spirit is present throughout their entire lives to help them deal with the powers of evil. A final passage rite moves the new Christian into deeper association with the church.

The final stage of initial faith formation, discussed in chapter 6, is instruction in vocation. All Christians are called to the vocation of living in their baptism. What does this mean in terms of one's gifting? How is a person to use his or her gifts in the church? How is a person to see work and vocation in the world as a service to God?

I am convinced that this approach to faith formation is applicable to Christian witness in every country around the world. While my application is to the North American culture in particular, the principles I cull from the ancient church are applicable worldwide—Europe, Africa, India, Asia, and Latin America. I challenge leaders from all countries and cultures of the world to take these biblical, ancient principles of evangelism and faith formation and translate them into their own culture. In this way we may serve the Great Commission and fulfill the challenge of the International Consultation on Discipleship to find a way not only to evangelize but to turn converts into lifelong disciples of Jesus Christ.

This fourfold process occurs over a six-month period. It has the advantage of giving the new Christian a strong start in the faith. This process should be seen as initial discipleship with the understanding that discipleship and growth in the Christian faith continues throughout life. This approach fulfills one of the goals of the International Consultation on Discipleship: "We will not water down the cost of discipleship in order to increase the number of converts. We acknowledge that part of making disciples is teaching people to obey everything that Jesus commanded."[7] What I adapt from the ancient church will do just that. It initiates new converts into a lifelong process of growth. Also, if those who are already disciples will walk through the process, it will inspire a deeper walk of faith. In this way the entire congregation will continuously disciple the entire congregation.

In part 2, "Cultural and Theological Reflection," I ask the reader to think about the culture of our post-Christian world as the context in which the church does faith forming. Then I explore the classical understanding of the message of faith and the meaning of the church and of worship. I ask for a return to a more substantive grasp of the faith.

In chapter 7, I argue that our culture is like that of the first three centuries in which the church emerged. Therefore, we can no longer assume people have a basic grasp of the Christian faith. Consequently, the local church needs to return to basics. Today many people long for a spiritual experience, but this longing is largely a narcissistic desire, a "what's in it for me" spirituality, an eclectic spirituality that chooses from this and that spiritual tradition to create a tailor-made spirituality (e.g., New Age spirituality).

Unfortunately, the predominant thought of the day regards Christianity as one more spirituality among many spiritualities. This spiritual relativism is so widespread that it is even being expressed in some churches. For example, I have a pastor friend whose daughter-in-law is a pastor. He tells me, "She loves Jesus, but she says, 'That's my way; others have their way that is equally valid.'" I argue that the uniqueness of Jesus Christ must be rediscovered as an essential feature of the Christian message. The very foundation of the Christian faith is "I am the way and the truth and the life" (John 14:6).

In chapters 8 and 9, I present three ancient theological themes that are woven into the fourfold process of faith formation. They are Christ as the Victor over the powers of evil, the church as the witness to God's saving action through Jesus Christ, and worship as a witness to God's mission accomplished in Jesus.

Note that I have placed the practice of making disciples first and the theological reflection second. This is in keeping with the principle that experience precedes reflection—an ancient principle that was reversed by modernity. Obviously, part 1 on practice contains theological reflection, and part 2 on cultural and theological reflection is relevant to the practical outworking of the process.

I urge you to begin with the practice. Don't spend a lot of time trying to "figure out" ancient-future evangelism. Take whatever time you need to review the resources and solicit a small group of people in your church who simply will do ancient-future evangelism. As you proceed, spend more time with the reflective part (2) and read some of the books suggested in the bibliography. In due time the process will flow naturally, the entire congregation will become involved, and the church will grow in depth and numbers.

Making disciples according to this biblical and ancient process is no quick fix. It is, to use the phrase popularized by Eugene Peterson, "a long obedience in the same direction." Eventually, and perhaps sooner than you think, the church will establish a rhythm in which the whole church disciples the whole church.

THE WAY NEW CHRISTIANS HAVE BEEN FORMED

In a recent doctoral course, "Worship, Evangelism, and Nurture," taught at Northern Seminary, I posed the following question: In the area of worship, evangelism, and nurture, what is your primary issue?

The seven students enrolled in the course were evangelical pastors from a broad variety of traditions—Free Methodist, African-American Baptist, United Church of Christ, Southern Baptist, Cumberland Presbyterian, an independent church, and Assemblies of God. The average age of these pastors was in the midforties; the average time in ministry was around twenty years. Remarkably, every one of these pastors pointed to a similar issue.

I asked for a one-sentence summary of the most significant problem they faced in ministry, and they wrote:

"Making real disciples is my primary issue."

"I need to slow down the process to baptism to make sure conversions are real."

"We enjoy a lot of Christian fellowship but have no sense of mission."

"My choir members are there to do music but little else."

"I need to move my people from low commitment to high commitment."

"I need my people to see conversion as a process."

"I need to get my people to real conversion and beyond."

As the course proceeded, it became clear that each pastor faced two problems. First, the various ministries of the church—worship, evangelism, discipleship, spiritual formation, and assimilation into the church—were compartmentalized. In the larger churches each division of ministry was represented by a different pastor—one for evangelism, another for Christian education, a music or worship pastor, and so on, depending on the size of the church. A common complaint that emerged was that each pastor worked alone without a great deal of his or her ministry integrated with the other ministries of the church.

The second issue was very similar to that of the conferees at the International Consultation on Discipleship. Why are there so many converts but so few disciples? Why is our church a mile wide but only an inch deep? How can we encourage growth and maturity in the Christian faith?

The following two questions are central to this book:

1. How can we get beyond compartmentalized programs and move to ministry?
2. How can we form new converts into disciples?

With these two questions in mind, I will trace the way the church has handled Christian formation throughout its history. First, I will show how the ancient church became a faith-forming community as it brought evangelism, discipleship, and spirituality together in a unified process of faith formation. Second, I will show how this ancient process of formation fell apart over the centuries. By understanding this history, the reader will be put in a better position to understand why an ancient-future evangelism needs to be recovered today.

Christian Formation in the New Testament Church

The New Testament church exhibited a unity between evangelism, discipleship, and Christian formation that provided a sequence of ministry. This ministry sequence moved new converts through stages of spiritual growth. Although the New Testament does not set forth a systematic and linear sequence of Christian formation in any great detail, here and there we see hints of early practices. Acts 2 contains several of these. Most obvious is the conversion process in "Repent and be baptized, every one of you, in the name of Jesus Christ for the forgiveness of your sins. And you will receive the gift of the Holy Spirit" (Acts 2:38). Later, the laying on of hands is associated with receiving the Holy Spirit (Acts 8:14–17). Worship on the day of Pentecost apparently included a time of instruction: "With many other words he warned them; and he pleaded with them, 'Save yourselves from this corrupt generation.'" Then, "those who accepted his message were baptized" (Acts 2:40–41). The content of this message is quite clearly stated: "Save yourself from this corrupt generation," but we are given no hint of the length of this instruction. Was it a paragraph or two containing a brief warning and instruction? Was it an instruction that took place over weeks or months? Paul refers to a pattern or form of teaching when to his readers in Rome he writes, "You wholeheartedly obeyed the form of teaching to which you were entrusted" (Rom. 6:17), but this would imply a delay of baptism. The example of the Ethiopian implies preparation in God's truth, followed by conversion and immediate baptism. While the sequence in the New Testament is not absolutely clear, the following elements of a process do emerge:

Hearing the gospel
Repentance
Instruction to flee the corrupt world
Baptism (a passage rite)
Reception of the Holy Spirit (signified by a rite)

The remaining portion of Acts is a picture of the early Christian community and its worship. What may be said about the Christian conversion and formation at this early date is that it included a change of heart and mind, rituals of Christian identification, instruction to flee the vices of the world, and a description of the Christian community and its worship.

It is clear from the Epistles that spiritual growth was expected of new Christians. The writer of Hebrews chides the community to which this letter is addressed: "Let us leave the elementary teachings about Christ and go on to maturity" (Heb. 6:1). Interestingly, the writer identifies the following as elementary teachings: "not laying again the foundation of repentance from acts that lead to death, and of faith in God, instruction about baptisms, the laying on of hands, the resurrection of the dead, and eternal judgment" (Heb. 6:1–2). These teachings sound similar to what surrounded entrance into the church at its very beginnings. Could this list refer to a body of knowledge and habits of life that are taught to young Christians in a process of spiritual formation?

In a 1940 study, Phillip Carrington, bishop of Quebec, England, claimed to have found a pattern in Ephesians, Colossians, James, and 1 Peter that stressed four points for all new Christians to observe. These four injunctions are summarized in the following phrases:

1. Wherefore putting off evil . . . *(Deponentes)*
2. Submit yourselves . . . *(Subjecti)*
3. Watch and pray . . . *(Vigilate)*
4. Resist the devil . . . *(Resistite)*[1]

Carrington concludes that because these four themes rose up in four New Testament books and in the same sequence, "there must be a reason for this." On the whole he concludes the vocabulary is "suggestive of a common catechetical tradition."[2] His study points to the fact that New Testament communities were developing a process of Christian formation to lead converts into an increasingly deeper commitment to the faith. The underlying feature of the New Testament process of discipleship is its holism. Today, if you wish your church to become a faith-forming community, it is necessary to establish a continuity between ministries of evangelism, discipleship, and spiritual formation.

Hebraic Holism and the Unity of Christian Ministry

A number of years ago a group of evangelical Hebrew scholars challenged Christians to stop using the term *Old Testament*. I heard this first from Ron Allen, professor of Hebrew Scriptures at Dallas Theological Seminary. His point was that by calling the Hebrew Scripture "old," we inadvertently regard it as passé and make it irrelevant to the Christian church. Allen and others called on evangelicals to recognize that, as Marvin Wilson writes, "the theology of the early church was Hebraic to its very heart."[3]

One dynamic feature of Hebraic faith is its holism. Our Western world has been shaped primarily by Greek thought rather than Hebraic thought. Greek thought separates, divides, and sees things in parts, whereas Hebraic thought sees things as whole and continuous. For this reason, when we approach the Scriptures and then our ministry, we need to "undergo a kind of intellectual conversion."[4]

Holism is an integration of faith and life. Faith is seen as a journey, a walk through all of life. Rabbi Joseph Soloveitchik says, "The Semites of Bible times did not simply *think* truth—they *experienced* truth. . . . We [Jews] are practical. We are more interested in discovering what God wants man to do than in describing God's essence. . . . As a teacher, I never try to solve questions because most questions are unsolvable."[5]

The Hebrew Scriptures and the New Testament documents are full of the imagery of life as a spiritual journey, pilgrimage, or walk. Enoch and Noah "walked with God" (Gen. 5:24; 6:9). The prophet Amos proclaims that those who "act justly and . . . love mercy and . . . *walk humbly* with your God" (Micah 6:8, italics added) are the ones who please God. Walking with God is the way of faith, the way of wisdom, the way of righteousness.

One of the most intriguing stories of the New Testament is the Emmaus walk (Luke 24:13–35). Here Cleopas and his companion (probably his wife) walked with Jesus, who unpacked the Scripture so that their hearts "burned" within. He then revealed himself as they ate bread together so that "their eyes were opened and they recognized him." They "got up and returned at once to Jerusalem" to tell the disciples gathered in the upper room that Christ was risen from the dead!

This New Testament story is thoroughly Jewish in the sense that it exhibits a holism. It's a story, not a series of abstract propositions. It's a walk, a journey that takes these disciples from despair to great joy. It is characterized by an unfolding from not knowing Jesus to encountering him in the Word and in breaking bread together to rushing forth to tell others. These walkers were seekers who became disciples and then became witnesses. The progressive elements of the story are one continuous stream of a deepening relationship with God, an awakening to faith and to their own ministry of being witnesses to the resurrection. In this journey they experienced a turning from dislocation to relocation in God—an apt image of the ministry we want to do in today's world! This is the model of a sequential and holistic process of formation connected with worship.

The Great Commission

A second example of sequential and holistic formation is evident in the Great Commission: "Then the eleven disciples went to Galilee, to the mountain where Jesus had told them to go. When they saw him, they worshiped him; but some doubted. Then Jesus came to them and said, 'All authority in heaven and on earth has been given to me. Therefore go and make disciples of all nations, baptizing them in the name of the Father and of the Son and of the Holy Spirit, and teaching them to obey everything I have commanded you. And surely I am with you always, to the very end of the age'" (Matt. 28:16–20).

Unfortunately, in the church today this passage has been lifted out of its context and given a life of its own. A proper interpretation of this passage places it back into its context of Matthew and the community to whom it was written.[6] The Hebraic holism that Matthew assumes can be seen in three sets of injunctions: (1) "all authority in heaven and on earth has been given to me"; (2) make disciples, baptize, and teach; and (3) "I am with you always."

The phrase "all authority in heaven and on earth has been given to me" places the making of disciples into the larger context of Christian truth. This includes the atonement, resurrection, ascension, and exaltation of Christ together with his lordship over all creation. It also encompasses the calling of the church to proclaim God's accomplished mission now and in the future *eschaton*, when the mission of God is completed in the new heavens and the new earth.

In the second injunction—make disciples, baptize, and teach—the Hebraic sense of holistic continuousness is expressed. These are not three separate categories of spiritual formation but three aspects of the whole calling and mission of the disciples of Jesus. The word *disciple* is the true description of the follower of Jesus. The word appears seventy-three times in the Gospel of Matthew, forty-six times in Mark, and thirty-seven times in Luke. The word itself means "to follow after," which implies the Hebraic concept of journey and walk. New disciples are to be modeled on the first disciples of Jesus, who were modeled after Jesus.

Matthew's concerns are both pastoral and missionary—"pastoral in that he holds up the first disciples as models for his own community as ideals to emulate, missionary in that he urges his community to 'make disciples' who should resemble the first ones."[7] Making disciples is clearly the overarching commission with baptism and teaching as part of the overall process. For Matthew, teaching is not divorced from disciple making; it is not a separate responsibility apart from discipleship, and teaching does not mean a mere intellectual framework. Instead, teaching "is a call for a concrete decision to follow him (Jesus) and submit to God's will."[8] "To 'believe,' to 'follow Jesus,' to 'understand' all contain an element of active commitment that flows into deeds."[9] The heart of discipleship in Matthew's Gospel is the Sermon on the Mount, in which Matthew expected the followers of Jesus "to live according to these norms always and under all circumstances."[10]

The third comment that expresses Hebraic holism is "Surely I am with you always, to the very end of the age" (Matt. 28:20). The presence of Jesus is not an occasional presence, nor is it dependent upon the disciples "making disciples." Rather, because Jesus is always and everywhere present to his disciples, they are empowered to be missional and to call others in the name of Jesus to a life of discipleship.

The Great Commission demonstrates that Jesus did not introduce various programs for evangelism, discipleship, and Christian formation. Instead, following in the tradition of Hebraic holism, Jesus taught that becoming a disciple is a process that takes place in a continuous way in the worship and community life of the church. This vision of a continuous walk is substantiated in the other Gospels, Acts, and the Epistles, but the study of these books and the communities they represent are beyond the limits of this writing.[11] Instead, I turn to the writings of the early church (second and third century) to provide more illustrations of the journey concept of making disciples.

The Unity of Ministries in the Ancient Church

The unity of the ministries of evangelism, discipleship, and Christian formation continued into the early church, especially the first three centuries. Careful attention was paid to this unity by the early church fathers.[12] Early church scholar Alan Kreider writes, "As I see it, in Christianity's early centuries conversion involved changes in belief, belonging and behavior in the context of an experience of God."[13]

A case in point is the conversion of Justin at about A.D. 130. A philosopher in search of truth, Justin set out from his home in Samaria to study under a "stoic, an Aristotelian, a Pythagorean, and a Platonist."[14] Yet in none of these did he find satisfaction. One day when he was walking by the sea, he encountered an old Jewish man, apparently a common person, who simply shared his own story of salvation. In response to this testimony, Justin was converted and transformed. He later spoke of this conversion as the opening of "the gates of light." Justin went on to be the greatest apologist for the Christian faith in the second century and died the death of a martyr.[15]

Justin's writings reveal the cycle of believing, belonging, and behaving that exhibits the making of disciples in the second century. In *The First Apology* he asserts the importance of belief when he describes those who are coming for baptism. He refers to them as persons who "are persuaded and believe that the things we teach and say are true"[16] and moves on to emphasize behavior in saying baptismal candidates are to "promise that they can live" by the teaching of the church. He warns that "those who are not found living as [Christ] taught should know that they are really not Christians, even if his teachings are on their lips."[17]

Justin is also the first noncanonical writer to provide us with a full insight into the worshiping community. He describes the reading and preaching of the Word and then adds elements of belonging to a community: fellowship that is characterized by common prayer, the passing of the kiss of peace, and the sharing of the Eucharistic meal.[18]

These unitive ministries of believing, behaving, and belonging are given in greater detail in the third century, especially in the writings of Hippolytus, a Christian leader in Rome. The commitment to make disciples and not just converts is evident in the development of a fourfold process of spiritual development that carried a person from a position of seeking through a process of hearing the Word and becoming a disciple, a deeper process of spiritual formation, and finally a process of assimilation into the full life of the church.[19] The terms Hippolytus used to describe the spiritual journey of making a disciple are *seeker, hearer, kneeler, faithful.* Between each of these four stages of spiritual formation is a passage rite, the final rite being baptism. Table 1 shows the process of evangelism, discipleship, Christian formation, and assimilation into the church in the late second and early third centuries.

Table 1: Spiritual Formation and Passage Rites

The Process	The Result
Stage 1—The Seeker	Christian inquiry
the rite of welcome	conversion
Stage 2—The Hearer	Discipleship
the rite of enrollment	commitment to become baptized
Stage 3—The Kneeler	Spiritual formation
the rite of baptism	full membership in the church
Stage 4—The Faithful	Active participation in the church

This journey of disciple making and Christian formation is clearly ordered around the cycle of believing, behaving, and belonging and is accomplished in the context of the worshiping community. Initial conversion brought the seeker into the church. Here the new believer spent considerable time as a hearer, learning how to live the Christian life. Next, the hearer moved to the stage of kneeler where he or she was instructed more deeply into the faith of the church, into the life of prayer, and into the reality of spiritual warfare. At the end of this period the believer was baptized into full membership in the church. Finally, in this state of belonging, the believer was known as faithful. In this fourth stage of spiritual formation he or she learned more about the mystery of worship, especially a fuller meaning of baptism and the Eucharistic meal.

This brief summary points to an intentional process of evangelism, discipleship, and Christian formation. The process of formation was not left to mere hope that the new converts would mature. Instead, the church's approach to new converts was to take them by the hand and walk them through an intentional, life-giving process of formation that assured they believed the faith handed down by the apostolic community, that they learned how to behave like a Christian, and that they became active participants in the new community to which they now belonged. Unfortunately, this unitive process gradually broke apart into a series of programs, until the concept of a process of formation itself became lost.

We now turn to a brief overview of the dissolution of the unity between evangelism, discipleship, and Christian formation in the Western church. This dissolution and the barriers it creates to making disciples of new Christians is one of the major challenges we face in today's church.

The Dissolution of the Ancient Process of Christian Formation

The unity between evangelism, discipleship, and Christian formation achieved in the early church gradually broke down over a long period of time. The full story of this dissolution is far too complex a subject for this writing. Consequently, I will refer to the highlights of the story and suggest readings in which the story is told in greater detail.[20]

The Conversion of Constantine: Christendom and the Dissolution of Ancient Evangelism

The first blow to the unitive process of conversion came through the conversion of Constantine. Constantine, in a battle with his rival Maxentius, reportedly saw a vision in which he was told to paint the sign of the cross on the shields of his soldiers. He won the battle and attributed the victory to the God of the Christians. From that time onward he favored the Christian faith. However, while viewing himself as a Christian and practicing prayers in private, Constantine did not submit to the church until the end of his life. He honored the Christians, gave them special privileges, and made an ostensible claim to Christianity without believing, behaving, and belonging in the way established in the first, second, and third centuries. For two decades "Constantine offered the world a new possibility of an un-baptized, un-catechized person who nevertheless somehow was a Christian—a Christian Lord who had not bowed his knees to the Lord of the Christians."[21] Instead, he waited until he was in his deathbed to submit to the church and its process of conversion. Unlike Justin Martyr's conversion, which was connected to an experience, Constantine's conversion appeared to be rote and mechanical, following the rules but missing the Spirit. In this way he modeled a new kind of Christian—one who proclaimed faith but did not have a life of faith within the church.

Second, by legitimizing the church, Constantine caused it to shift from the counterculture model of the previous centuries to one that had a new place in society. It was now not only common but beneficial to be a Christian. Soon benefits were given to church leaders, buildings were provided for meeting places, and the careers of civil servants were enhanced if they were Christian. What was once a hostile environment for Christians now became an inviting climate for Christians and a hostile place for pagans and Jews.

Infant Baptism: A New Paradigm

Consequently, both the meaning and process of conversion changed in the fourth century. Society had become Christianized, so to speak. Therefore, baptism shifted from adult baptism to infant baptism, and the process of Christian formation now had to occur after baptism.

Augustine is a case in point. He reports how he was received into the church as an infant, which then admitted him immediately to the position of being a catechumenate (one under instruction in the faith). According to this system he was now a baptized person who needed to be instructed before becoming a full member of the church. During the time as a catechumenate, Augustine could hear sermons but not receive the Eucharist. He then submitted to the church, was instructed in the faith, and went on to become one of the great fathers of the church.

The process of Christian formation had changed. Prior to Constantine, the process was conversion, rigorous training in discipleship and Christian formation, followed by baptism and full admittance into the life of the church. After Constantine, however, the rise of infant baptism challenged the process and resulted in the breakdown of the process itself. This shift to infant baptism laid the groundwork for the developments in conversion and discipleship in the medieval era.

Medieval Christendom: Baptismal Regeneration

The shape of conversion and discipleship in the medieval era was determined by the rise of the institutional church and by the sacramental system of salvation. Both the theology and process of conversion had developed into a fixed understanding and form. Following is a summary of the medieval process of conversion and discipleship:

- Salvation was first administered to infants at their baptism, which forgave original sin and gave the infant the gift of the Holy Spirit (baptismal regeneration).
- A first confession was made at about age seven in preparation for the child's first communion.

- The first communion was administered.
- The child was confirmed either before or immediately after first communion. It was thought that confirmation provided an increase of the Holy Spirit, spiritual maturity, and a readiness to do battle with evil as the child was made a "little soldier" of the faith.
- When the child, or now adult, sinned, the sacrament of penance was available to restore a right relationship with God.
- The Eucharist provided a continued relationship with God. (In the late medieval era a rule was made that the Eucharist must be taken once a year.)
- The sacrament of unction, administered by the priest, was the final sacrament of salvation provided on the deathbed.[22]

In the high medieval period of the thirteenth century, it was taken for granted that all people were Christians except for Jews and some pagans. Christianity, it was argued, was the very air breathed in this Christian society. One was born into an atmosphere of faith. The Christian context that assured eternal life was the cycle of life from baptism at birth, confirmation in early adolescence, the availability of penance and the Eucharist, a marriage lived sacramentally, the affirmation of God's grace at death, and even burial in the churchyard.

In this system, especially in the High Middle Ages, many had faith and lived lives of sincere devotion to God. The great cathedrals are testimonies to the faith of the artisans who built these majestic buildings. Art, literature, music, philosophy, and even town planning all issued around the church. In many ways the High Middle Ages marked the transformation of society, a crowning achievement of leaders who were deeply devoted to God and to making society into a visual and tangible experience of heaven.

Yet the sacramental system of faith and spirituality, which looks good on paper, did not last. In the two hundred years before the Reformation, the system became abused, much of the papacy and clergy became immoral, salvation was sold through indulgences, and the church became corrupt. Attempts were made to renew the church, and here and there monks, friars, and priests like John Wycliffe and Jan Huss were able to break through the spiritual impasse. In many ways their leadership paved the way for the Reformation.

The Reformation Era: Catechetical Innovation

The Reformation of the sixteenth century did not occur in a vacuum. The whole world was undergoing a paradigm shift. The old medieval world with its political, economic, educational, artistic, and religious structures was passing through enormous changes.

Two changes that specifically bear on our topic of evangelism and Christian formation were the Renaissance and the invention of the Gutenberg press. The press made it possible for the Bible—a book that had been forbidden to be read—to be printed and distributed. The Renaissance revived education, and what was once a highly illiterate society was now characterized by educated people who could read and write. The age of print had arrived.

So how did print change the matter of evangelism and Christian formation? The Catholic system of salvation taught that the practice of baptism and confirmation conferred an "indelible character on the soul, i.e. a kind of spiritual seal."[23] The sacraments made a person a Christian. However, in this system of salvation there seemed to be no emphasis on how the sacramental gift of salvation was nurtured into an experience of living faith. The sacraments worked the work of faith without the necessity of personal response.

Luther, like the Catholics, retained infant baptism but restructured its nature in light of the central doctrine of justification by faith. Luther believed that salvation comes from God in the church because of the work of Jesus Christ. The Holy Spirit calls us to faith through the gospel as it is proclaimed in the Word and embodied in the water of baptism. Infant baptism is "a most fitting paradigm of God's gracious justifying act." An infant is "a model of complete dependency and trust" because an infant has nothing to offer—"no works, merits, or personal decisions." Instead, "an infant witnesses to Luther's theological understanding that salvation is entirely God's act alone."[24] Thus Luther wrote in the *Large Catechism*, "Baptism is valid, even though faith be lacking. For my faith does not constitute baptism but receives it."[25]

Luther also had a lively sense of how Christians are called to live in their baptism. The work of the Holy Spirit through baptism was to produce an identification with the death and resurrection of Jesus into which the person had been baptized. In the *Holy and Blessed Sacrament of Baptism* (1519), Luther wrote that baptism "is nothing other than a rehearsal for death itself and, as a consequence, Christian life is to be a daily death to sin and resurrection to life, a remembering of and living out of baptism which will come to its ultimate fulfillment only in the final death when the old self—the old Adam—dies completely in order to be raised up to life forever."[26]

This lively faith is generated by the Spirit through the instruction in faith that comes *after* baptism, *before* confirmation, but also throughout life in the church. To assure this lively faith Luther introduced the *catechism* (the word means "instruct"). The catechism was made possible because of the invention of print and the widespread ability to read and write. Luther's catechism, known as *Kleiner Katechismus,* was the greatest contribution to Christian education and personal spiritual formation of the sixteenth century. It was published in 1529, and within forty years more than one hundred thousand copies had been sold. Other catechisms appeared as well in the Reformed community of Calvin and in the Catholic church as a result of the Counter-Reformation.[27]

The purpose of the catechism is made clear in the preface to Luther's *Kleiner Katechismus* of 1529: "It is necessary to make the pupils and the people to learn by heart the formulas chosen to be included in the little catechism, without changing a single syllable. As for those who refuse to learn word by word, tell them they are denying Christ and are not Christian. Do not accept them at the Lord's Supper. Do not let them present a child for baptism. . . . When the children know these texts well, they must also be taught their meaning, so that they will understand what the words mean."[28]

The catechism is essentially a way of inculcating Christian doctrine. Its emphasis is on knowledge and personal commitment to knowing the truth. The positive feature of the catechism is that it teaches the Christian faith, a matter neglected in the medieval era. The negative feature of the catechism is that children become subject to intellectual faith and lose the spirit of being "a creative and mystical Christian."[29]

The negative impact of the catechism has reverberated down through history in the Protestant tradition. The spirituality of the medieval mystics and the spirituality fostered by the sacramental system when it was at its best was now supplanted by intellectual knowledge. The rejection of everything Catholic then led to the Protestant notion that knowledge and spirituality were the same. For nearly five hundred years the spirituality of Protestantism has been expressed in the quest for knowledge. This quest found a happy partner with the emphasis on reason in the modern period. In the postmodern era, however, where knowledge is not enough, there is a longing once again for the disciplines that produce a spirituality rooted in the mystical and sacramental traditions.

Calvin, like Luther, maintained infant baptism, and the Reformed movement produced its own catechism. Both Luther and Calvin rejected the sacramental system of spirituality. They both retained the notion of God's grace made available through baptism (with some nuances of difference). They also retained confirmation but emphasized that the person to be confirmed had to learn the basic knowledge of the faith summarized in the catechism and had to express a willingness to embrace that faith personally.

Because both Luther and Calvin continued to work out of a Christianized-society mind-set, evangelism was still attached to infant baptism. Then Christian formation was identified as knowledge affirmed at confirmation. For both Luther and Calvin, the Eucharist was viewed as a rite of continuous nourishment. The approach to evangelism and Christian formation among the Reformers is summarized in table 2.

Table 2: Conversion and Discipleship among the Reformers

The Sacraments	The Result
Step 1—Infant Baptism	Evangelism
Step 2—Catechism	Teaching the knowledge of faith
Step 3—Confirmation	Affirmation of commitment
Step 4—Eucharist	The rite of continued nourishment

The Reformation also produced the Anabaptists, who were very different from Luther or Calvin.* The Anabaptists modeled themselves after the church of the first three centuries. Consequently, they rejected the state church, infant baptism, and the entire sacramental system. For this they were resoundingly persecuted, even by Lutherans and Calvinists.

For Anabaptists evangelism and spirituality were based on a repudiation of the state and society. This was followed by a personal, radical choice to follow Jesus demonstrated by adult baptism and life lived in an alternative community of faith. Here they followed the disciplines of Christ through voluntary submission to the leadership of the Christian community. This radical discipleship spread rapidly throughout Europe. Thousands were martyred for their faith, but it was a light that no one could put out. The Anabaptist way cut a path into the future that shaped aspects of the free church tradition (as opposed to that of the state church) until the present day.[30]

Table 3: Anabaptist Conversion and Spirituality

The Choice	The Commitment
Step 1—Adult Baptism	Evangelism arising out of personal choice
Step 2—Discipleship	Life in the Christian community under the discipline of the church

*Anabaptists proper include groups such as the Amish and Hutterites, who live totally apart from the common culture, to Mennonites and Brethren, who live in varying degrees within the culture. They are known primarily for their pacifism and compassionate social action.

This Anabaptist model gave rise to the insistence on the distinction between church and state and argued for a countercultural Christianity. Since the collapse of a Christianized society, a new appreciation of the Anabaptist principles has become widespread among Christian cultural critics. From the seventeenth century to about 1950, the Anabaptists were largely ignored by the Protestant establishment. During the Enlightenment the Anabaptists continued their way of life with little to no interaction with the established church. They were even ignored by the free church, which was the beneficiary of their martyrdom and the convictions for which they died.

The Enlightenment: Shift to Reason and Experience

The Enlightenment, which began in the eighteenth century, introduced a new worldview that was to undermine vestiges of Christian formation that still remained in the Reformation churches. First, the Enlightenment was characterized by the supremacy of reason. The revolutions in cosmology, epistemology, and science suggested that the world worked like a machine and was understandable. This worldview led to several new developments. For one thing, Christianity became privatized; this was especially true with conversion, which was seen as an experience, not subject to rational inquiry. On the other hand, conservatives, using the primacy of reason, argued that Christianity was a rational, logical, coherent system of truth that could be proven to be true. Consequently an apologetic approach to Christianity developed. It was an intellectually driven cognitive view of the faith that neglected the disciplines of spiritual formation and favored what Josh McDowell has aptly called the "evidence that demands a verdict" Christianity.[31]

Second, the supremacy of reason separated all aspects of life into distinct disciplines. Each subject constituted an era of inquiry in and of itself. For example, the compartmentalization of disciplines is reflected in education. In high school, students attend six or seven classes a day studying each subject for fifty minutes at a time. These programs of study isolated one inquiry from another and treated subjects as though they were independent of each other. The same mentality impacted the church, which developed various programs of ministry. A case in point may be Sunday school organized around studies designed for particular age groups, each rooted in a particular field of inquiry. Generally, because of the rational nature of Sunday school, these studies have little to do with disciplines of spiritual formation.

During the Enlightenment, the use of the catechism continued to dominate Reformational Christianity as a way of instructing people in the faith and through that method achieving Christian formation. This form of learning for the most part has had an independent life of its own and has not fostered a process that integrates the church, its worship, discipleship, Christian formation, and the like into a coherent whole. Christian evangelism, discipleship, and spiritual formation were seldom if ever intentionally integrated with each other in a way that made a total impact on the life of faith.

A second kind of Christian formation emerged during the Enlightenment. A revolution against *mind-oriented Christianity* was initiated by the *heart-oriented Christianity* of the pietists of the seventeenth century, the revivalists of the eighteenth century, and the missionary movement of the nineteenth century. These movements introduced the concept of a conversion experience that could be connected to a specific date. This new method can be best illustrated by the ministry and writings of John Wesley and the evangelical awakenings in England and America.

In order to understand Wesley and these movements in general, a word needs to be said about an alternative way of knowing that had been introduced in the seventeenth century. Both Luther and Calvin had emphasized that a relationship with God was based largely on right knowing. By the seventeenth century, the emphasis on right doctrines produced a Protestant orthodoxy, which in its worst expression was an embrace of orthodox teaching without the transformation of life.

A reaction grew against this Protestant scholasticism. It asserted the primacy of feeling and called for a passionate Christianity not only marked by right doctrine but also a feeling of forgiveness, a commitment to piety, and a Christian life concerned for the poor and needy. John Wesley had an experience of faith in which he felt his heart "strangely warmed." This experience propelled him into an active ministry of mass evangelism. Followers of Wesley popularized the "invitation" or altar call to a personal, life-changing decision to be a follower of Jesus.[32]

The evangelical revivals of Wesley set into motion another kind of Christianity that has remained in conflict with the mainline Christianity of Luther and Calvin. These two streams of Protestant Christianity—Reformational and evangelical—are characterized by a highly conflictual understanding of evangelism and spiritual formation. This conflict is evident today, although unknown in its detail to many practitioners of the faith. Briefly speaking, it is an objective versus a subjective approach to the faith and Christian discipleship. The objective process, taught by the Reformers and their successors, emphasizes how God's grace works to save humanity. The subjective approach, espoused by many evangelicals, emphasizes how personal faith takes hold of God's grace. Table 4 illustrates the difference.

Table 4: Reformation Salvation Process Compared to the Evangelical Process

Objective Christianity: The Process of God's Grace	Subjective Christianity: The Process of Human Faith
Imputation God gives salvation as a gift.	*Regeneration* A person experiences the new birth.
Justification Man embraces this gift through faith expressed in baptism and confirmation.	*Justification* The feeling of forgiveness, an assurance of salvation in the heart
Sanctification The Christian thankfully lives out salvation in a life of holiness and works of mercy.	*Sanctification* The Christian consciously dies to sin and chooses to be resurrected to the new life.

The emphasis on the subjective side of salvation among the evangelicals led Wesley to develop a process of salvation and spiritual formation that bears a close resemblance to the process established in the third century. Table 5 gives a brief outline of the process of salvation and spiritual formation practiced by Wesley and his early followers.

Table 5: The Wesleyan Process of Salvation

The Process	The Results
Step 1—Preaching Directed toward the entire congregation	Evangelism, repentance, and faith
Step 2—Societies Class meetings for pastoral care	Small groups that embody the way of salvation
Step 3—Society bands Smaller groups for discipleship and spiritual formation	Societies were divided into subgroups to handle various conditions such as relapse or pursuit of Christian perfection.

This form of spirituality remained dominant in Wesleyan evangelicalism throughout the nineteenth century. Twentieth-century evangelicalism, rooted in the fundamentalists' debates of the first part of the twentieth century, was dominated by the Reformed paradigm but mixed up with the evangelistic preaching style originating with Wesley and continued by Charles Finney, Billy Sunday, and Billy Graham. However, the twentieth-century evangelists did not continue the process of Christian formation initiated by Wesley and expressed in the societies and society bands.

Twentieth-century evangelicalism failed to develop any patterns of ministry that integrated the various disciplines of Christian formation into a coherent whole. Instead, it developed parachurch movements that sought to fill the void left by the traditional church. These movements range from children, youth, and college ministries to business groups, prayer walks, men's or women's groups such as Promise Keepers or the small group movement, as well as small- and large-scale evangelistic rallies. These parachurch movements all supplemented the ministries of the church, which continued to offer various programs for children, youth, men, women, singles, and married people. Consequently, evangelical Christianity has been characterized by many movements—some that evangelize, others that disciple, still others that seek to provide spiritual awakening, commitment, and social action. Yet there has been a noticeable lack of any attempt to put into place a process that brings all these elements together in the ministry of the local church. The hunger for unitive ministries of Christian formation is now beginning to emerge, as seen in the small group movement of many churches. These small groups, however, are not yet fully integrated with Christian formation.

The Challenge to Recover Unity of Ministries

The new understanding of a highly complex and interrelated world challenges the notion that we can view the world in separate parts. The world is now seen in its total complex unity. This unified vision of reality has resulted in a new emphasis on interdisciplinary studies. Church leaders now see the need to bring all the ministries of the church together in a coherent whole. Evangelism, discipleship, Christian formation, and assimilation into a full, conscious, and active participation in the church is not achieved through a series of unrelated programs in a willy-nilly way. Rather, church leaders are already experimenting with models of ministry that bring together what were once different ministries and programs into a process of spiritual formation.

Furthermore, the rise of a secular and pagan society, the emergence of the New Age Movement of spirituality, postmodern pluralism, and relativism have created a new cultural situation in which the church speaks the faith. So, where do we go in the twenty-first century with the ministries of evangelism, discipleship, and Christian formation?

The Future

A new common understanding is emerging. Rick Warren, pastor of Saddleback Community Church in Saddleback, California, has articulated the future in these words: "Instead of focusing on growing a church through programs, focus on growing people by setting up a process, based on God's purposes, that enables people to become what God intends for them to be. If you will do this, the growth of your church will be healthy, balanced, and consistent."[33] In keeping with his advice to other ministers, Warren has set up a baseball diamond pictorial process for conversion and spiritual formation that looks like this:[34]

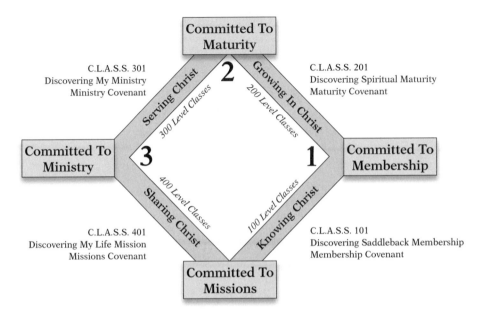

The Saddleback Life Development Process

Rick Warren and hundreds of churches influenced by his process are seeking to undo the dissolution of the unity that rightly belongs to evangelism and Christian formation. In part 1, I take the reader back to the well-developed model of the early church that was designed for a pagan and pre-Christian world, which is in many ways like our own world. It speaks to the newly awakened sense that evangelism must result in discipleship and Christian formation.

Conclusion

The International Consultation on Discipleship put its finger on a crucial issue: Current models of evangelism do not make disciples. I have pointed out the early church's emphasis on the unity between evangelism and the ministries of Christian formation and have briefly sketched the dissolution of the unity between evangelism and Christian formation throughout the history of Christendom.

Finding a process for Christian formation has now become a burning issue among evangelicals around the world. How are we going to meet the challenge? The burden of *Ancient-Future Evangelism* is to say that clues to the future are found in the third-century model. Of course, we cannot simply pick up the ancient model and drop it unchanged into the twenty-first century. Instead we need to draw from the principles at work in the ancient model and adapt these principles to Christian formation in a post-Christian culture. In part 1, I identify these principles and apply them to Christian formation in our present post-Christian world.

Table 6: Christian Formation in the New Testament and Early Church

Theme	Its Manifestation
Hebraic holism	Faith is seen as a journey, a walk throughout life.
The Great Commission	Jesus did not introduce "programs" to make disciples. Becoming a disciple is a lifelong process.
Second- and third-century discipleship	The process has developed into four stages and three passage rites.

Table 7: The Dissolution of the Ancient Process of Christian Formation

Event	Effect on Christian Formation
The conversion of Constantine 311 A.D.	The introduction of infant baptism brought about the breakdown of adult conversion and the ancient process of Christian formation.
Medieval Christendom 600–1500	The sacramental system of salvation—grace is given from infancy to the grave. It works objectively without an emphasis on proper Christian discipleship.
Luther and Calvin 1500–present	Continued with infant baptism, developed the catechism, and retained confirmation.
The Anabaptists 1500–present	Restored adult baptism and accountable discipleship in the church
The Enlightenment 1750–1950	Christian formation is seen as intellectual acquiescence.
Wesleyan evangelism 1750–1900	The primacy of feeling; the born-again experience; small group accountability
Twentieth–century evangelicalism	Mass evangelism separated from any intentional process of Christian formation in the local church. Various forms of Christian formation emerge in parachurch groups.
Twentieth–first–century evangelism	The International Consultation on Discipleship calls for the restoration of a process of Christian formation that restores the unity of Christian ministries.

Questions for Discussion

1. Take time to review the history of Christian formation. Firmly fix this history in your mind so that your discussion can freely flow from one period of history to another.
2. Locate the current theology and practice of Christian formation employed in your church in the historical period in which it emerged.
3. Compare your current model with the process of Christian formation in the New Testament period and in the early church.
   a. What can you learn from Hebraic holism?
   b. What can you learn from the Great Commission?
   c. What can you learn from the practice of the early church?
4. How does the analysis of the International Consultation on Discipleship pertain to your church? (See appendix 4.)
5. What steps should you take to return to the model of the early church?

PART ONE

THE PROCESS OF CHRISTIAN FORMATION

In the chapters that follow I argue that conversion happens within community. We encounter Jesus through the church as it embodies truth. Conversion is not merely embracing an intellectual idea; it is taking one's place within the body of people who confess Christ and seek to live out the kingdom of Jesus. Thus one does not merely know intellectually but one knows holistically in community.

I also show how knowing God in community requires a participation in the language of the community. This is why a church does not say, "Let's find out the needs of people and create a church that meets their needs." Unconverted people don't know their need in any comprehensive way. They don't have the language to identify their sinful condition nor to describe the redemption that is brought by Jesus. They need to learn the language of faith—a language that can only be known through an association with the church. This is why the road to evangelism and Christian formation takes place within the church. Through the various stages of evangelism, discipleship, spiritual formation, and Christian vocation, the church teaches the converting person the language necessary to enter into a vital relationship with God. If a church takes away its language of faith by simplifying it to the point that it has no common meaning, the church has destroyed the linguistic tools it needs to provide the converting person with a language that provides meaning and depth to personal spiritual formation. Disciplines of Bible study, worship, prayer, and spiritual warfare are learned disciplines, and they are learned only while using the language of the church.

Finally, I show that the process of discovering a new language within the church creates a paradigm shift. The converting person's way of perceiving reality takes a huge leap into a new way of believing, belonging, and behaving. The story of God creating, of a world falling away from God, of God's involvement in the history of Israel, and of Jesus rescuing the world at the end of history is a radical way of seeing and being. It is a paradigm totally opposite to that of secularism, the New Age Movement, Islam, or any other religion of the world.

This paradigm is learned within the community—through teaching, worship, prayer, spirituality, and discussions about values, the family, the nation, and the history of the world. It is for this reason that I suggest the church borrow the ancient process of Christian formation and adapt it for the twenty-first century. Its way of knowing and the content that it teaches is consistent with the faith of the ancient church and is especially relevant to the epistemological shift from the modern dependence on reason to the current recognition that knowing takes place in community as we learn its language.

Knowing God, becoming a disciple, learning spirituality, and finding your Christian vocation all occur in community. This is the central theme of ancient-future evangelism—a theme set forth in the following chapters.[1]

2

MAKE DISCIPLES

The International Consultation on Discipleship defines discipleship as a "process that takes place within accountable relationships over a period of time for the purpose of bringing believers to spiritual maturity in Christ. Biblical examples suggest that discipleship is both relational and intentional, both a position and a process."[1] This lifelong process of making disciples begins with evangelism but continues in increasingly deeper levels of understanding and commitment. Throughout history this process has been given different names. In the early church it was seen as union with God accomplished by the Spirit. In the medieval church the process was related to the sacramental system and referred to as the infusion of God's grace. The Reformers recovered the language of justification and sanctification and made a distinction between the event of salvation and the process of discipleship. The pietists and revivalists introduced the language of the new birth and a life of dying to sin. In these languages and in others employed throughout history, there is a consensus that the making of a disciple is a process. Discipleship can be defined, then, as the *process of making disciples*. But what is a disciple?

The Biblical Understanding of Discipleship

Today in many evangelical circles, it is popular to make a distinction between a convert and a disciple.[2] Converts, it is assumed, are believers, church members, and even workers in the church who have not taken the second step into discipleship. Does the usage of the word *disciple* in the Scripture warrant this distinction between a converted person and a disciple?

The word *disciple* is used 230 times in the Gospels and twenty-eight times in Acts. It is "the primary term used in the gospels to refer to Jesus' followers and is a common referent for those known in the early church as *believers, Christians, brothers/sisters, those of the way*, or *saints*." Furthermore, "individual disciples are always seen in conjunction with the *community of disciples*, whether as Jesus' intimate companions or as the church."[3]

According to the New Testament usage of the word, a convert is a disciple. The disciple is one who receives Jesus as his or her personal Savior, becomes a member in the church, the body of Christ, and commits to living under the reign of Jesus in the way Jesus taught. At first the disciple may know very little. He or she may not know the full story of God's redeeming work from creation to re-creation. He or she may not know the full extent of what it means to submit to the lordship of Christ. The disciple may not know how to pray, how to read the Scriptures, how to live a Christian life. He or she may not be aware of how to deal with evil, how to live in a countercultural way, or how to be an active member of the body of Christ. The disciple may not know what his or her gifts are or how to use them in the life of the church. He or she may not know how to see all of life as Christian vocation.

Why is this so? It is because the new disciple is an infant in the faith. He or she is now brought into the church, not as an adult with a mature perspective, but as an infant who needs to be nurtured and brought up in the faith. Just as we need to care for and nurture our offspring by bringing them into a healthy family where we love them, nurse them, and train them through the stages of life into maturity, so also the church is to do the same for the newly born spiritual infants. The new convert is a disciple just as much as a newborn baby is a human being. Most new disciples know almost nothing about the faith. They must be instructed and formed.

For example, some time ago a friend who had become a Christian late in life was telling her story. She had been divorced and remarried several times before her conversion. When she converted, she was living with a man who was not her husband. He also converted at the same time. Shortly thereafter they began attending an evangelical church. Soon they decided to get married, so they made an appointment to see the pastor. During the conversation with the pastor, whom they had not met nor talked with until then, it came up that they were living together. Immediately the minister said, "Don't you know that Christians don't live together until they are married?" The couple, having come from a secular background, were amazed at his comment. They had never heard of such a thing. However, because they were converted and were now disciples of Jesus, they immediately moved apart and did not cohabit until they were married.

A convert is a disciple. Whatever Jesus calls disciples to do, they do. The issue is not "now that you are a convert, you may want to consider being a disciple." A convert is a disciple, and a disciple will do what the Master wants. Yet the new disciple has to learn how to be a disciple, and that is the work of the church—to make disciples.

The issue raised by the International Consultation on Discipleship is that many evangelical churches have been successful in converting people but unsuccessful in forming Christians into disciples. This problem raises the question: Is a convert who does not become a disciple a true convert? This is a theological question beyond the scope of this writing. Regardless of how one may answer the question, all would agree that a new disciple should become a lifelong disciple. Can a new disciple grow into maturity without a process in the local church? However one answers that question, most would agree that having a process in the church to make disciples is better than not having a process. Yet most evangelical churches do not have an intentional process for forming disciples.

Becoming a disciple, just like becoming a fully mature human being, takes time, takes the involvement of committed people, and takes a process of growth and development that is intentional and well worked out. The problem we are dealing with is not only the problem of individual Christians who don't grow but the problem of local churches that don't have a process for nurturing and growing new Christians into mature disciples. The International Consultation on Discipleship said as much when it decried, "Our zeal to go wider has not been matched by a commitment to go deeper."[4] Evangelical churches are good at reaching out and bringing people in through conversion, but they are not nearly as good at nurturing and bringing to maturity the new Christians. A desperate need exists for a process that takes the new disciple by the hand and leads him or her toward maturity.

The Ancient Process of Making Disciples

The early Christians who lived in a world very much like our own developed a process to form new Christians into disciples.[5] Numerous Gentiles with no background in faith, no sense of community or of ethical behavior, flooded the church. The process of making disciples began in the first century and developed over a period of time into a well-worked-out, step-by-step process of Christian formation. This process was fully developed by the end of the second century and is detailed for us by Hippolytus in his work *The Apostolic Tradition,* which is generally dated around A.D. 215.[6]

This process, referred to in chapter 1, was based on four formative steps and three passage rites. Here is a summary using the language of the early church:

Inquiry
   Rite of Welcome
Catechumenate
   Rite of Enrollment
Purification and Enlightenment
   Rite of Baptism
Mystagogue

My concern is to recover the spirit of this process, not its letter. The purpose of ancient-future evangelism is to adapt the ancient process into an evangelical witness in the twenty-first century. Before I begin the task of showing how this ancient process can provide an answer to the dilemma raised by the International Consultation, I need to survey the structure, the content, and the passage rites of the ancient process.

First, the *inquiry,* in which a person was known as a seeker, was for the purpose of setting forth Jesus' call to "follow me!" The emphasis was on the cost of discipleship. Becoming a disciple in the first three centuries was to put one's life into danger because of the illegitimate status of the Christian faith in the Roman Empire. Christianity was unlike other religions. Other religions did not practice exclusivity; you could belong to as many religions as you wanted. Not so with the Christian faith. It was not one of many ways but *the way!* Consequently the inquiry was a time for the church to make certain that the person to be admitted to discipleship was willing to affirm that Jesus is the only way. New converts committed to a *metanoia,* a turning away from all other religions, a turning to Jesus Christ alone as Savior and embracing his way of life as the exclusive way of discipleship.

This decision on the part of the seeker was ratified by the *rite of welcome,* which signaled the beginning of postconversion discipleship. This ritual was characterized by a renunciation of all false religions (all the religions of the Roman Empire), receiving the sign of the cross (an invisible tattoo that indicates you now belong to Jesus), and a formal ritual of walking into the body of believers and taking a seat among them as a sign of entrance into the church.

Now the new disciple was a *catechumen*. The word means "one who is instructed," and it signified a period of time to be instructed in the faith and in the Christian life. In the worship of the church these catechumens were dismissed after the sermon. While baptized Christians remained for the Eucharist, the catechumens gathered in a place where they could reflect on the sermon. Led by a mentor, they were instructed in matters of the faith and in the development of Christian character. This process continued for two or three years.

The passage rite from the catechumen stage to the next stage was called the *rite for the enrollment of names*. The purpose of this rite was to declare the disciple's intent to become baptized. The rite also declared the church's recognition that the disciple had demonstrated a true conversion to Jesus as the only way, a willingness to walk in the way, and sufficient progress in discipleship and the formation of the Christian faith to be baptized.*

The next stage, known as *purification and enlightenment,* occurred during the weeks preceding Easter, the time the church eventually called Lent. This short period (six weeks) was a time for intense spiritual formation with an emphasis on how the Christian struggles with the powers of evil. Theologically the theme was on spiritual warfare. The accent was on Ephesians 6:12, "For our struggle is not against flesh and blood, but against the rulers, against the authorities, against the powers of this dark world and against the spiritual forces of evil in the heavenly realms." A special feature of the worship of this short period was the prayer time known as the "scrutinies." The soon-to-be-baptized disciples were brought forward in worship before they were dismissed. Hands were laid upon them, and special prayers were offered asking God to protect them against evil and to form within them the character and resolve of a disciple who lives in the victory of Christ over evil.

On Easter morning, at what was known as the great paschal vigil, the disciple was baptized. The service began on Saturday night and consisted of four parts: lighting of the fire in the dark, readings of Scripture, baptism, and Eucharist. The lighting of the fire in the dark signaled the bursting forth of the resurrection. The readings of Scripture occurred through the entire night and included the creation through the fall and the promise of redemption. In the morning at the rising of the sun the new disciples, now formed in the faith, were baptized. They were immersed three times—in the name of the Father, the Son, and

---

*Catechumens were viewed as Christians prior to baptism. They were told that if they were martyred for the faith, their blood was their baptism. Baptism was delayed to give the new disciples time to know what they were committing themselves to be and to give the church time to teach the cost of discipleship. There are no statistics available on what proportion of people dropped out of the process prior to baptism.

the Holy Spirit. After baptism they were signed with oil as the symbol of receiving the Holy Spirit (based on Ephesians 1:13). Baptism was a festive moment in the life of the church and in the process of discipleship. It symbolized a full and complete identification with the death and resurrection of Jesus Christ. They know who Jesus is. They are willing to follow Jesus even to their death—and many did! After baptism, the fourth part of the Easter service was the celebration of the resurrection in the Eucharist. For the first time the new disciple was invited to stay for the entire service of worship and join the other baptized Christians in the celebration of the Lord's Supper.

Now the new disciple entered a phase of disciple training known as *mystagogue*. During this time, which took place during the seven weeks of Easter, ending with the day of Pentecost, the new disciples were led in reflection on the mystery of faith, especially the meaning of baptism and Eucharist, and they were taught to care for the poor and needy.

Translating the Ancient Process of Discipleship into Evangelical Churches

It is obvious that the ancient process *made disciples*. The questions we must ask now are: Can we translate this ancient process into our evangelical churches? If so, how? The conviction of *Ancient-Future Evangelism* is that we can translate the spirit of this ancient process of discipleship into a local church. We can do so by adapting its structure, its content, and its passage rites.[7]

Adapting the Structure of the Ancient Process of Discipleship

The fourfold structure of the ancient process is very simple:

1. Evangelize
2. Disciple
3. Spiritually Form
4. Assimilate

The ancient fourfold structure of discipleship that occurs over an extended period of time assumes a developmental understanding of discipleship.

I grew up with the impression that once a person became a Christian, growth in Christ was a natural outcome of faith and there was no need of a more formal process. I may have been wrong in assuming this, but the local church communicated this conclusion by the absence of an intentional process of Christian formation.

The International Consultation on Discipleship suggests that the lack of Christian formation among conservative churches is a worldwide phenomenon. The International Consultation bemoans Christians who are not "different from the culture around them" and Christians who are "not living lives of biblical purity, integrity and holiness." This has "resulted in a lack of power in the church to impact our cultures."[8] Should we be asking what kind of process we can put into place that will form new Christians into committed disciples?

The New Testament writers expected growth and development in the Christian life. In the great passage in which Paul states that salvation is by grace and not of works, he reminds Christians that "we are God's workmanship, created in Christ Jesus to do good works, which God prepared in advance for us to do" (Eph. 2:8–10).

The early church fathers, like Paul, saw the Christian life as growth and development. Gregory of Nyssa, referring to Moses, wrote, "Moving ever forwards, [he] did not stop in his upward climb. . . . He constantly kept moving to the next step; and he continued to go even higher because he always found another step that lay beyond the highest one that he had reached."[9] Gregory admonishes disciples to "never stop rising, moving from one beginning to the next, . . . for the desire of those who thus rise never rests in what they can already understand; but by an ever greater and greater desire, the soul keeps rising constantly to another which lies ahead."[10]

The fathers of the ancient church recognized that discipleship is a matter of the heart, the will, and the intellect. For example, Cyril of Jerusalem, who was very concerned for the intention of the heart, admonished those in the process of Christian formation with these words: "It is the sincerity of your resolution that makes you 'called.' It is of no use your body being here if your thoughts and heart are elsewhere."[11]

This is the spirit of the process of formation. It does no good to simply go through the motions. Formation in every stage is a matter of the heart's intention. As congregations approach this material and think of its possible adaptation in the local church, they should not think of it as "another program." Turning the process of spiritual formation into a program will undermine its very purpose. It is a spiritual process, a process that the church sets in motion to engage the heart, the mind, the will, indeed the whole person, in a lifelong commitment of discipleship.

The process is clearly rooted in the biblical mandate to *make* disciples. It thoughtfully works out a way to introduce new Christians to the whole picture of what it means to be a disciple, and it provides a context that integrates new Christians into the whole life of the church. The result is a community of people committed to growing together as disciples.

Adapting the Content of the Ancient Process of Discipleship

Second, the content of ancient evangelism and discipleship is thoroughly biblical. Therefore, the emphasis of each stage of development can also be followed.

1. Evangelize into the gospel of Jesus Christ.
2. Disciple into the church, its worship, its Scripture, its disciplines.
3. Spiritually form into the ethic and lifestyle of faith.
4. Assimilate into the church through a discovery of gifts, the Christian vocation of work, and caring for the poor and needy.

The content of this fourfold process in today's world can be seen as an initial six-month introduction to the content of the Christian faith. It has the advantage of giving a new disciple a strong start in the faith, and it fulfills one of the commitments of the International Consultation on Discipleship: "We will not water down the cost of discipleship in order to increase the number of converts. We acknowledge that part of making disciples is teaching people to obey everything that Jesus commanded." The broad scope of the process introduces the new disciple to the demands of discipleship and calls them into a commitment to growth in Christian knowledge, to Christian belonging, and to living the Christian ethic, not for a short season but throughout all of life. I will not develop this further at this point because chapters 3 through 6 assume the structure and explore the content of each stage.

Adapting the Passage Rites of the Ancient Process of Discipleship

The ancient process of Christian formation includes three passage rites that can be easily translated:

1. a passage rite of conversion
2. a passage rite between the stages of discipleship and spiritual formation
3. a passage rite between the stages of spiritual formation and Christian vocation

Most evangelical churches do not use rites of passage to symbolize growth and development in the faith. However, most evangelical churches do use baptism as a passage rite that expresses conversion. In each of the stages of conversion, discipleship, and spiritual formation, I will suggest what passage rites may be used and how to use them. At this point, let me suggest why passage rites from one stage to the next should at least be considered.

THE SIGNIFICANCE OF PASSAGE RITES

For more than a century evangelists and pastors have used the *invitational ritual* at the end of crusades and worship services. This ritual is *extrabiblical*. There is no place in Scripture that lays down the invitational process of asking people to raise their hands for prayer and receive the assurance of salvation. The same can be said for the process of seeker evangelism. The process of coming to a seeker service in anonymity to reflect on the claim of Jesus has no biblical precedent. The use of ritual in conversion is a matter of style that relates to the cultural setting in which evangelism is done.

However, the origin of ritual in conversion and disciple making is found in the New Testament rite of baptism (Acts 2:38) and the laying on of hands to receive the Holy Spirit (Acts 8:15–16). In spite of the presence of these New Testament passage rites, some may ask, "What is the value of a passage rite? Why do we do passage rites at all?" It should be noted first that life is full of rites. We celebrate everything from birth to death with rituals—baby showers, birthdays, weddings, graduations, and anniversaries. Special milestones in life are all accompanied by rituals that mark these significant transitions.

One may want to consider the use of passage rites in light of current communication theory. Since the time of print, which has had a significant impact on the history of the Protestant church, the use of words has dominated our worship and religious experience. They speak truth and reflect reality. However, Peter Roche de Coppens suggests that rituals "deal with the intuition, with imagination and with emotion rather than with thinking sensations or the will."[12] Obviously the Christian faith is word oriented, but the use of symbol and ritual does not ask the faith to be any less verbal, only more symbolic. Word and ritual go together. The word communicates to the verbal and cognitive side of the person, whereas the symbol or ritual communicates to the emotive side of the person. The issue is not either/or but both/and.

Arnold van Gennep has identified three very important aspects of rites of passage. "A complete scheme of rites of passage theoretically includes preliminal rites (rites of separation), liminal rites (rites of transition), and post liminal rites (rites of incorporation)."[13] Baptism is the supreme rite of initiation into the Christian faith because (1) it expresses renunciation of Satan and all that is associated with evil, (2) it expresses a transition from one state of being to another, and (3) it expresses incorporation into Jesus Christ, his death and resurrection, and life in the church.

CONVERSION AND THE RITE OF BAPTISM

Conversion is a *metanoia*, a turning away from sin and a turning to Jesus Christ. The ritual that signifies this dramatic change is baptism. Those who heard and received the message at Pentecost asked, "Brothers, what shall we do?" (Acts 2:37). The answer was "Repent and be baptized, every one of you, in the name of Jesus Christ for the forgiveness of your sins. And you will receive the gift of the Holy Spirit" (Acts 2:38). Conversion and baptism are bound together. Certainly Paul saw the unity between the two. The teaching on justification by faith in Romans 5 is immediately connected to Paul's great exposition on baptism in Romans 6. Baptism is the sign of our identity with the death and resurrection of Jesus Christ. "We were therefore buried with him through baptism into death in order that, just as Christ was raised from the dead through the glory of the Father, we too may live a new life" (Rom. 6:4).

It appears from Acts 2 and from other examples in the New Testament church (such as the Philippian jailer, the Ethiopian eunuch, and Paul himself) that baptism was administered shortly after the profession of faith. Yet in the early church and as early as the *Didache*, an early noncanonical document that describes early Christian practices of ministry, which French scholars date around A.D. 50, there was a delay in baptism.[14] This delay was probably established because some converts fell away from the faith due to having no background to the meaning of their commitment either in believing, behaving, or belonging. This was the case for Simon (Acts 8:9–25) and the falling away of believers dealt with by the writer to the Hebrews (Heb. 5:11–14).

The problem of converts falling away from the faith was not only an early church problem but one addressed by the International Consultation on Discipleship. "Our zeal," the International Consultation states, "to go wider has not been matched by a commitment to go deeper."[15] Should today's evangelical community adopt the early church practice of delaying baptism in order to establish a process of Christian formation before baptism? How a local church answers this question will determine the use of passage rites in the process of evangelism and Christian formation.

The ancient church, for reasons cited above, did delay baptism. A similar case to delay baptism in today's post-Christian world could also be made. The delay of baptism provides time for a convert to be formed by the church and become more deeply versed in what it means to become a Christian—believing in Jesus, belonging to the church, and behaving according to the Christian ethic. Does the Scripture speak to the issue?

New converts from a Jewish background in the New Testament era were probably baptized immediately because they already had the experience of believing, belonging, and behaving. Faith in Jesus as the fulfillment of the messianic desire and transfer into the church, where the ethic bore great similarity to the Hebrew ethic, was a natural transition to make. Yet for the Gentiles who had no background or experience in believing, belonging, or behaving, the transition into the Christian faith, church, and ethic was much more of a change than it was for devout Jews. This raises the question of whether baptism should be delayed for unchurched, post-Christian converts to provide time for them to be clear about what they are embracing.

The norm in the first three centuries of the church was adult baptism. Baptism was delayed for Gentiles until a person had demonstrated Christian character and a firm commitment to the faith. But should a church delay baptism today? Each local church is free to establish its own policy based on its tradition and the consensus of its people. In either case, whether the choice is to baptize immediately or to delay baptism, the process of conversion, discipleship, spiritual formation, and Christian vocation need not be interrupted. Instead, what will change from church to church will be the use of passage rites.

- Some churches will choose to delay baptism and follow the ancient pattern of rites that lead up to the final passage rite—baptism.
- Some churches will choose to do immediate baptism followed by other rites.
- Some churches will choose to do immediate baptism with no additional rites.
- Some churches that baptize infants will need to reconstruct the fourfold pattern of Christian formation and the use of rites in keeping with the commitment to infant baptism.

These four approaches to baptism represent the evangelical spread. Any attempt to solve the problem and suggest a uniform practice among the churches is beyond the scope of this writing. Therefore, I simply will suggest how passage rites may be used in each option.

At the end of each chapter presenting a stage of development, I suggest a variety of passage rites that might be used. While I personally consider passage rites to be an important part of the process, I present the four stages of conversion, discipleship, spiritual formation, and Christian vocation as the essential stages of Christian formation and allow for the use of passage rites as optional. Equally committed Christians will disagree on the use of passage rites. Allowing each church to determine the use of passage rites for itself permits all churches to concentrate primarily on the stages of Christian formation.

For example, let me tell you the story of a church that chose to have only one rite—the rite of baptism—but festooned the occasion more by connecting it with symbols that are not used in the other rites of passage. This church has a very active presence in its neighborhood. The pastor was a former homeless person who believes the church is open to all—and all come. Because of their open-door policy and because they are such a joyous community of formerly shipwrecked people, people come from every walk of life—doctors, motorcycle riders, lawyers, dancers, former prostitutes. In this church people are frequently being saved and incorporated into the life of the church but without much ceremony.

When I arrived to do some lectures, the pastor asked some questions about my seminar. I explained the process and then told him I would be doing some passage rites to illustrate the movement from conversion to discipleship and so on. He shuddered and looked rather dismayed. "We don't do rituals here," he said. Not knowing what to say, I responded, "You'll like these rituals."

A few weeks after my workshop the assistant pastor called me. "Bob," he said in an excited voice, "we celebrated a couple more conversions this week. In today's worship I did a converting rite with baptism and it just blew them away. The whole congregation was in tears."

The rite he created for that situation included phrases for the new convert to repeat such as:

"I renounce the works of the evil one."
"I renounce all the works of sin."
"I trust only in Jesus Christ for my forgiveness and salvation."

He then asked the congregation if they would support these new converts in prayer and fellowship, to which the entire congregation shouted, "I do!" Then the new converts were presented with a cross and a Bible with appropriate comments about the importance of these symbols and their place in the Christian life. Finally, the new converts were invited to sign their names to a parchment containing the words of their commitment. The associate pastor said, "The entire congregation was moved by the ceremony."

Conclusion

I have provided a brief overview of the four stages of development, the content, and the rites for those stages. Each local church should feel free to adapt these principles in a way that is compatible to their own tradition. (See appendix 1, "Various Sequences for the Stages and Passage Rites," and appendix 2, "Descriptions of the Passage Rites," for suggestions of when and how congregations can use the passage rites.) The ancient process does not need to be treated legalistically and translated into our post-Christian culture in a wooden and mechanical way. Let each local congregation catch the spirit of the ancient model and listen to how the Spirit leads them to apply the model in their cultural setting.

What is of ultimate importance is having a process of discipleship so that the church not only has a vision for reaching out but a way of making disciples.[16] The four aspects of this process of discipleship are examined more fully in the next four chapters.

Table 8: The Making of a Disciple

Theme	Comments
Biblical understanding of *disciple*	All converts to Jesus are disciples. Discipleship is not an option.

Ancient process for making a disciple	Inquiry
	   rite of welcome
	Catechumenate
	   rite for the enrollment of names
	Purification and enlightenment
	   rite of baptism
	Mystagogue

Translating the ancient process for today	Evangelize the seeker
	   first passage rite
	Disciple the hearer
	   second passage rite
	Spiritually form the kneeler
	   third passage rite
	Assimilate the faithful into the church
	Christian vocation

Questions for Discussion

1. Do you agree that a convert is a disciple? Why or why not?
2. How do you respond to the ancient process of Christian formation? The sequence of the stages? The goal of each stage? Each passage rite?
3. What challenges would your church face if it chose to translate this ancient process for today?
4. What benefits would your church receive by adapting the ancient process for today?
5. Is there a willingness to consider its use?

EVANGELISM

On a recent trip I fell into conversation with the man sitting next to me on the plane. After discussing the faith he asked, "If I want to pursue the Christian faith further, what do you suggest I do?" I immediately told him to find a good church in his neighborhood, and then I added, "You should also read the Gospel of John." "Gospel of John," he responded, "what is that?" I briefly explained the origin and meaning of the four Gospels and spoke of them as eyewitness accounts of the life, ministry, death, and resurrection of Jesus Christ. "I've never heard about those books!" he exclaimed. "I'll be sure to get them and read them. They sound fascinating."

This man was a middle-aged, well-educated president of his own company. He was an example of the "secular but interested in spiritual things" kind of person who lives in every strata of our present society.

Today's evangelism is being done in a society characterized by the secular/spiritual paradox. Many people are secular but influenced by the persuasive spirituality of society. Yet, like this man, they know little about the Christian faith. Christians and the church must come to grips with this reality and find ways to evangelize the secular but spiritually inquisitive seeker in our post-Christian world. In *The Secularization of the World,* well-known sociologist Peter Berger affirms that secularization has "provoked powerful movements of counter-secularization."[1] Therefore, Berger challenges the assumption that only those religious institutions that adapt to secularization will survive. According to his data "religious communities have survived and even flourished to the degree that they have *not* tried to adapt themselves to the alleged requirements of a secular world. To put it simply, experiments with secularized religion have generally failed; religious movements with beliefs and practices dripping with reactionary supernaturalism . . . have widely succeeded."[2]

Clearly, a new social and cultural situation has emerged. It can be summarized this way:

1. We live in a world that is postmodern and secular.
2. A reaction against secularism has resulted in the rise of a distinct group of people longing for a supernatural understanding of the world.
3. Consequently we are dealing with a paradoxical situation in which the world is secular yet longing for a supernatural spirituality.

Evangelism in today's world must take this paradox into consideration. Where do we look for a model? I have already argued that the time of history most approximate to our post-Christian era is the first three centuries of the church. Ancient society was secular in that it knew nothing about the God of the Bible, about the incarnation, death, resurrection, and return of Jesus, about the church and its vision and ethic. It was religious in that nearly every person embraced some form of religion—philosophy, a mystery cult, Judaism, or an aberration of Christianity such as Gnosticism. Yet it was in this secular/spiritual context that Christianity flourished and spread. What was it that caused Christianity to grow rapidly in those first three centuries? What can we learn from them that will ignite our witness today?

Antonia Tripolitis responds to these questions with three insights drawn from her studies of the church in antiquity.[3] First, she tells us that "an important factor was its openness." Christianity was simply accessible. The cults, in contrast, were "secretive and exclusive." Mithraism "excluded women" and the philosophical schools of religion "made salvation an intellectual accomplishment."[4]

Second, Tripolitis found that "intransigence was also an important factor for its success."[5] Christians would not budge on their exclusive message that salvation is through Jesus Christ alone. The pagan religious counterparts were inclusive and fluid. Pagans were always willing to compromise their message and adapt it to include other religions. Consequently they offered no certainty because they offered many ways to salvation, whereas Christians presented their faith in Jesus Christ as "the way."

The exclusive nature of the Christian faith led to a third cause of its success: it created community. Tripolitis refers to the unique nature of Christianity as a "close-knit, organized and disciplined community with its members bound together by a common rite, a community of life, and by their common danger." This "gave its members a true sense of belonging, a sense of security." Yet this community of Christians did not constitute an "in group" who cared only for its members. These Christians "gave freely to the poor, the hungry, and the thirsty; they visited the sick and the imprisoned, and clothed those that had no clothing." Tripolitis concludes that "Christianity's sense of community and its universal charity were a major reason, if not the most important single reason, for its growth and subsequent victory over the empire."[6]

The early church teaches us three principles for evangelism in a secular/spiritual culture: we must be open to all; we are to preach, teach, enact, and live an exclusive Christian message; and we need to create a community that not only looks after its own but cares for the needs of the world. In chapter 8, I deal with the second of these three matters—the uniqueness of Christ as the one true message in the midst of the plurality of religions. Therefore in this chapter I will concentrate on the need to reach out and the need to build a welcoming community as two necessary steps for a local church evangelism in our post-Christian world.

Reach Out

First, how does a church reach out in today's secular/spiritual world? Drawing from the example of the early church, today's church must be a hospitable community of people who reach out through social networking.

Amy Oden, a student of hospitality in the early church, writes that we find two important themes on hospitality in early Christian literature. "The first is that Christians must recognize themselves as strangers in the world. The second is that Christians must recognize strangers as Christ."[7] She quotes the sojourner theme found in the second-century document *Epistle to Diognetus*, which describes the Christians' sense that they belonged ultimately to another world. Diognetus describes Christians as "citizens [who] share in all things with others, and yet endure all things as if foreigners. Every foreign land is to them as their native country, and every land of their birth as a land of strangers."[8]

The second motif of this paradox is that every stranger to the Christian community is in fact Christ. Oden cites Chrysostom, the bishop of Constantinople in the fourth century, who urges Christians to receive strangers and help the poor. "Have a room," he admonishes, "to which Christ may come. Say, 'this is Christ's space. This building is set apart for Him.' Even if it is just a basement and tiny, He won't refuse it. Christ goes about 'naked and a stranger.' It is only a shelter he wants . . . greater are the benefits we receive than what we confer. He does not require you to kill a calf, but only to give bread to the hungry, raiment to the naked, shelter to the stranger."[9]

The research of sociologist Rodney Stark into growth in the early church agrees with the insights of Antonia Tripolitis and Amy Oden. He argues that "the basis for successful conversionist movements is growth through social networks, through *a structure of direct and intimate interpersonal attachments.*"[10] Stark also observes that "new religious movements mainly draw their converts from the ranks of the religiously inactive and disconnected and those affiliated with the most accommodated (worldly) religious communities."[11] Robin Lane Fox, another sociologist and student of the early church, writes, "Above all we should give weight to the presence and influence of friends. It is a force which so often escapes the record, but it gives shape to everyone's personal life. One friend might bring another to the faith. . . . When a person turned to God, he found others, new 'brethren' who were sharing the same path."[12]

Social networking in a post-Christian world will primarily happen where people eat together in homes of Christians and in neighborhood communities where faith is shared. Eating has always played a central role in the Christian faith.

Jesus' own eating habits are frequently highlighted in the Gospels. His behavior "recreated the world. . . . Instead of symbolizing social rank and order, it blurred the distinctions between hosts and guests, need and plenty. Instead of reinforcing rules of etiquette, it subverted them, making the last first and the first last."[13] In this way Jesus both embodied the kingdom and prophetically anticipated the kingdom. Furthermore, there were no preconditions to eating together. Conversion was no prerequisite to fellowship at a common meal with Jesus. Instead, conversion became a consequence of eating with Jesus. Likewise, in the early Christian church eating together continued to be a vital part of community (Acts 2:42–47). Today a crucial aspect of evangelism must be that of eating together. It is the primary context for establishing relationships that lead to discussion of things that matter. The success, for example, of the Alpha course in reaching people is that friends and neighbors gather around food.

David Fitch, pastor of Life on the Vine Church in Long Grove, Illinois, argues that because eating is a primary point of contact, "postmodern evangelism will take place in the believers' homes." Here "evangelism incubates in the climates of hospitality, in the places of conversation, posing questions, listening to the strangers in our midst."[14] In keeping with this philosophy of ministry, Fitch has trained the congregation of

Life on the Vine to focus "upon disciples meeting strangers and sharing life with them in their backyards, around their tables at their place of need."[15]

Postmodern evangelism will also occur in neighborhood communities in which seekers are included "in groups of twenty to thirty people who meet together monthly to share fellowship and discernment."[16] In these groups where people converse and relate to each other in casual and personal ways, evangelism will take place as the unchurched are exposed to Christians who embody the faith and discuss ways to be authentically Christian in today's world.

Engagement with non-Christians through social networking that results in home gatherings around the table and an invitation to be part of a neighborhood community is the crucial first step in evangelism. This first step is illustrated in the example of Pantego Bible Church in the suburbs of Dallas.

Randy Frazee, pastor of Pantego Bible Church, wrote *The Connecting Church* to explain how they have created community in the post-Christian culture.[17] He set forth a model that churches committed to connecting to secular/spiritual people should seriously consider. Frazee's church was originally built around the small group ministry. Many, however, found "small groups were not achieving authentic community."[18] They set out to discover why community was not being achieved and how they might overcome the obstacles to genuine community. They found three major obstacles to community throughout the warp and woof of the Western way of life—individualism, isolationism, and consumerism.

Individualism has spawned the "me culture." This individualistic attitude that says "I'll think what I want, do what I want, go where I want, and be responsible to no one but myself" has crept into the church and is reflected in the highly personalistic religion of many Christians. Frazee countered this individualism by calling on the church to "once again come together around shared beliefs and values."[19] He gained this conviction from the research of early church historian Wayne Meeks. Meeks observes that one peculiar aspect of "early Christianity was the way in which the intimate, close-knit life of the local groups was seen to be simultaneously part of a much larger, indeed ultimately world wide movement or entity."[20] Frazee asserts that a common purpose of the church that transcends individualism is found in an authority structure that allows for accountability—a creed that produces "a shared understanding of its beliefs and practices," traditions that pass down the authority and creeds, standards that "define what is expected of people," and a clearly defined mission "that brings the individuals of a group together and knits them into a cohesive family."[21] This Bible church pastor then urges, "We must adopt from the ancient church what a follower of Christ looks like. Incorporating these common beliefs, practices and virtues into the lives of people must constitute the central purpose that draws the Christian community together."[22]

Frazee identifies the second major obstacle to community as the isolation engendered by modern life. He points in particular to the places in which we live. He draws on the recent sociological studies that show how our modern buildings and sprawling suburbs prevent relationships from happening.[23] The American dream of the wide boulevard, manicured lawn, big house, huge supermarket, car-dependent life or of the inner-city, high-rise apartment has undermined the community once experienced in cities, small towns, and rural areas where people visited with each other on the front porch, sidewalk, local grocery store, and gas station. What has been lost, claims Frazee, is spontaneous relationships, availability of people for each other, frequency of being together, common meals, and geographical locations where people live close to each other.

So what is the solution to the problem of isolation? *Building neighborhood churches.* Frazee quotes Robert Wuthnow, "When your friends all know each other because they are in the same group, you are more likely to experience the tendency toward personal consistency that fellow believers refer to as *discipleship*."[24] Frazee notes that "a series of disconnected linear relationships will never achieve this; it takes a cohesive circle of friends." The church that would evangelize must "rediscover the ancient concept of *neighborhood*."[25] Neighborhood is related to place. The church, to be missional, must define the boundaries of its ministry and create neighborhood communities within those boundaries where the sense of community can grow in a natural and spontaneous way. This is the old "parish principle." If you lived in a particular neighborhood, you became a member of the church that served that neighborhood. During the last fifty years this concept has broken down because of the rise of the isolated suburb and access to a wider world through the car and the road system. But the missional church seeks to minister to the neighborhood.

For example, on a recent trip to Louisville, Kentucky, I visited Sojourn, a church that is seeking to be missional.[26] The pastor told me, "We have a distinct neighborhood we serve. Within this neighborhood we have established a number of small house church groups—and that's where the life of the church really happens—and then we all come together on Sunday to worship together in a public way."[27]

The third problem Frazee identifies that inhibits community is consumerism. The driving principle of consumerism is "rights over responsibility." "In this system," he writes, "the pursuit and protection of one's rights always wins out over one's responsibility to his or her neighbor."[28] Consumerism undermines community because it makes us overly independent, distorts our views of the people who are around us, leads us to a preoccupation of defending our property and rights, results in an indifference to the poor and needy, and inspires us to accumulate more things. How do we deal with this matter of consumerism? Frazee finds the answer in being more countercultural, in learning how to make our possessions more available to others. This kind of community will create a life opposite to the lives we now live. It will foster an interdependency, an intergenerational life, a concern for children, and a sense of responsibility for each other.[29]

This kind of church community that Randy Frazee envisions is a new paradigm for most of us, but it is the paradigm of the past and the future. The church that addresses the issues of individualism, isolationism, and consumerism by building a "neighborhood house community witness" will be the church that effectively evangelizes and makes lifelong disciples. It will fulfill the three characteristics of the early church that grew rapidly in number and depth. It will be open and accessible to everyone, it will have a clear set of beliefs and lifestyle, and it will achieve a sense of community. Once that kind of church has been set in motion, the task of evangelism can be addressed in a new way.

Build Community

The second step for evangelism in the post-Christian world is for the church to build an intentional community. In the modern world the most dominant approach to evangelism was mass evangelism. The scene is familiar: The well-known evangelist comes to town. Cooperating churches organize their people to bring friends. The unsaved are presented with the sacrificial work of Jesus on their behalf. An invitation to receive Jesus is given. Those who respond to the invitation are instructed to read the Bible, pray daily, and go to the church of their choice. Certainly many people came to Christ with this method begun by John Wesley and continued by Charles Finney, Billy Sunday, and Billy Graham. (Statistics show that .5 percent come to the church through crusades.)[30]

Then came seeker evangelism. Again, the scene is familiar: Train Christian people to develop genuine friendships with the unchurched. Create a megachurch that doesn't look like a church. Establish a facility that has a place and ministry for everyone—youth, singles, children, married. Develop a seeker service in which unchurched people can come, be anonymous, and take their time to consider the claim of Christ on their lives. When they become converted, graduate them to involvement in a small group ministry and the midweek worship and Bible study. Find their gifts and release them to work in the church. This model has enjoyed enormous success throughout the world.[31]

The model for the missional church differs from mass evangelism and from seeker evangelism because missional evangelism locates the focal point of evangelism in a community of people who embody in their lives the message and reality of the Christian faith. Let me explain. In modern forms of evangelism, the faith is primarily verbalized and communicated directly. For example, an evangelist will proclaim the Good News in a rally, or one-on-one evangelism will have as its goal explaining the gospel in a simple format such as the *Four Spiritual Laws*. The seeker church provides time and anonymity to consider the message. The missional church, on the other hand, evangelizes primarily by *immersing the unchurched in the experience of community*. In this community they see, hear, and feel the reality of the faith or "catch" the faith. The social context of the neighborhood community is that of extended family and friends. According to recent statistics, 79 percent of people who convert and enter into the church do so because of personal contact with a relative or friend.[32]

This shift to evangelism through community is based on an epistemological shift that has taken place in the rise of postmodernity. David Fitch addresses the epistemological shift into postmodernity,[33] and his argument needs to be understood by those who are committed to evangelism in this secular/spiritual world. Postmodernity rejects two main assumptions of modernity. The first is that the scientific method results in objective truth. The second is that truth is available through reason. Both of these assumptions lie behind twentieth-century evangelism.

Both mass evangelism and seeker evangelism exhibit confidence in the power of reason and science to convince a person to believe in Jesus. Christianity was the verdict demanded by the evidence. This method "tacitly trains the new initiate to depend upon science as a higher source of truth than scripture."[34] The alternative way of knowing truth in the postmodern world is to be "convinced of truth through participation, not consumer appeals; through wholly lived display, not reasoned arguments."[35]

Modern forms of evangelism emphasize words and presentations that appeal to the mind's reasoning powers or to the will driven by emotions. But in postmodernity, as communication specialist Pierre Babin points out, "the aim of evangelization becomes the Christian community, and its main medium is also the Christian community. Recognition of this is essential in defining our pastoral options: the medium is the community of believers themselves. It is their dynamic faith, their life-style, and the witness they bear to having been healed and saved by Christ."[36]

Postmodern evangelism is not so much an argument but a display. Fitch writes, "We display what these words mean in the way we live and worship so that its reality, once displayed, cannot be denied, only rejected or entered into."[37] For this reason "the church becomes the post modern portal to truth. It becomes the basis for evangelism."[38] Consequently the "onus is on the church to become the center of living truth."[39] This view of truth, Fitch claims, "will invigorate the importance of historical traditions as carriers of living truth."[40] In this sense evangelism not only invites people into a local community but a community that is shaped by a tradition of worship, discipleship, Christian formation, and vocation that is rooted in the teachings and practices that go all the way back to Jesus and his disciples. New Christians do not enter into a community that reinvents the Christian faith for every new generation. Instead the local community in which faith is embodied and lived is a community with both long-standing historical connections and relationships and a worldwide web of people in every culture and geographical area around the globe.

Evangelism through an Immersion in Worship

In addition to being a community that embodies truth, the church is also a community that proclaims, sings, teaches, and enacts truth. This happens in worship. In worship the unchurched are immersed in truth as the community remembers God's great acts of salvation, discerns the ways God's presence and power are now available, and points to the eschatological vision of the new heavens and earth. Here, in worship, personal stories of faith and conversion are linked with the story of God's saving acts, past, present, and future.[41]

What kind of worship evangelizes? To answer this question, the nature of worship itself must be addressed.

Worship is not a program. In programs the Christian faith is communicated primarily through verbal means of print or broadcast. Truth is presented to people who are asked to consider it, believe it, and act on it. In postmodern settings, as in the early church, truth that is embodied by the community is *rehearsed* in worship and symbolized in the rites and symbols of faith. This kind of worship calls for participation in the truth it proclaims and acts. Faith is birthed in participation.

I have frequently used the term *rehearse* to describe what happens in worship. Some have objected to the term, arguing that to say that worship is a rehearsal of our relationship with God is to say that it is getting ready for the real thing, not actually participating in the relationship worship implies. Not so. I use *rehearse* in the sense of a continual experience of the relationship. For example, in the act of eating with family or friends, in the very context of gathering, in the words that are said, in the gestures made, and in the symbols employed, a rehearsal of relationship occurs. So it is with worship. Worship is relationship in motion. Worship is a dialogue between divine action and human response. It rehearses a relationship between God and man as it is done.

The divine side of worship is the story that worship tells and enacts. The story moves from creation through the fall, the incarnation, death, resurrection, and ultimate redemption in the new heavens and the new earth. Worship gathers the people to hear and enact this story in the prayers, songs, testimonies, preaching, and actions of worship (such as baptism and the Lord's Supper). When worship is rightly done and rightly understood by the people worshiping, they become immersed in the gospel through participation. The human side of worship is to intend it. The worshiper opens himself or herself to be shaped by worship and to learn how to live it. In this way worship that says and does truth is the public window not only to the church but to the seeker's experience of the truth.

For example, preaching, which is an act of worship, is directly related to conversion. People, even those who have been believers for a long time, need to hear that everything that needs to be done to make us acceptable to God has been done by Jesus. He is the sacrifice for our sins, the Victor over the powers of evil, the one who shows us how to live life, and the one who eternally intercedes for us before the Father. In these themes it is made clear that salvation is a gift of God's grace. We are justified by grace through faith and by no merit of our own. Good preaching also presses the other side of this message and calls people to respond, to believe, to embrace, and to become lifelong disciples of Jesus committed to live out his teachings.

This kind of worship—worship that proclaims and enacts the gospel so that our relationship with God is rehearsed—speaks to our postmodern way of knowing. This kind of worship is not designed to be an entertaining program or a rational presentation directed toward the mind alone. Instead, in its simple and authentic way, the dialogue that takes place in worship between God and the worshiper invites the worshiper to enter into a relationship with God.

For example, Karen Howe of Florida writes about this kind of experience: "I became a Christian sitting in a pew, experiencing worship. It wasn't the sermon that did it. No one presented me with the plan of salvation or led me in a prayer of commitment (though that did come later). I simply basked in the presence of God as the worship service progressed around me, and when I left the church I knew that God had entered my life. He was alive. I had encountered Him. That day I was born in the Spirit."[42] The experience of conversion is not dependent on an invitation at the end of the service. Rather, it happens because the unchurched are in church as a result of relationships in which they see faith embodied. Through an association with authentic Christians, truth is assimilated. At some point the Christian faith is internalized and a personal commitment to Christ as Lord and Savior is made public. This may happen in a direct moment of *decision* within worship or with a friend, or conversion may be more gradual and *dawn* on a person who wakes up one day to exclaim, "I'm a Christian!"

In this process Christian witness is not dependent on arguments or evidence. (Although reason may be used without being reliant upon it, reason is not what gives credibility to Scripture.) The Holy Spirit testifies to truth; God has not established reason or argument as the means of conversion. From the very beginning of the church it has always been the testimony of the Spirit that validates the Word and leads a person to Christ. Paul clearly states, "You were justified in the name of the Lord Jesus Christ and by the Spirit of our God" (1 Cor. 6:11). He brings the work of Christ and the work of the Holy Spirit together. John Calvin remarks on this point: "The Holy Spirit is the bond by which Christ effectually binds us to himself."[43] In the post-Christian world in which the rational methods of modernity are suspect, the reliance on the Holy Spirit to bind a person to Christ has emerged as a primary factor in evangelism.

Somewhere along this trajectory, through an association with people who embody truth and a worship that proclaims and enacts truth, a genuine experience of faith in Christ will be acknowledged. A conversion takes place by the power of the Spirit.

For example, a few years ago a single woman with a young son moved next door to us. Over a period of time we became good friends with her. Although we did not have a neighborhood group with which she could associate, we invited her and her son into our lives. They often came for coffee or a meal, and we included them in family outings. In all these situations we incorporated our faith into our discussions and perspectives on life. She frequently asked serious questions. We answered them but never pushed her toward a decision. One day around our kitchen table as we drank coffee and talked, there seemed to be an intensity about her conversation. I didn't say, "Do you want to receive Jesus now?" Instead I simply asked, "You want to go to church with us, don't you?" She responded without hesitation, "Yes, I really do." That Sunday she began going to church with us. She soon confessed Christ. To this day she continues in the faith. Considering the description of conversion I have given above, it is fair to ask, "What is the nature of conversion?"

The Nature of Conversion

The International Consultation on Discipleship bemoans the current evangelical state of superficial conversions. It calls the evangelical church to establish a means by which converts may be led into greater spiritual depth. In order to meet the challenge of the International Consultation, we need to see conversion as a start in the faith. The disciples left everything for the call to follow Jesus, and then for three years they were taught and discipled by him. This New Testament conversion included belief, belonging, and behavior.

An early church historian and theologian, Gustave Bardy, claims, "The idea of conversion in the sense we give it today, remained for a long time, perhaps until the arrival of Christianity, utterly foreign to the mentality of the Graeco-Roman world."[44] Evangelists and early church theologian Michael Green agree that conversion prior to Christianity was not known in the Greek or Hellenistic world. He points out that the idea of conversion introduces three new realities into the first century:

1. Christian conversion required belief. In pagan religions one was not asked to believe in a god but to perform duties and rituals for the god.
2. Conversion to Christ implied ethical transformation. In Roman culture there was no connection between religion and behavior. You could follow this or that god and behave any way you wanted.
3. Conversion in the Christian sense implies devotion to Jesus and a belonging to his community. This also was strange to the Hellenistic mind. The mysteries were only open to those who belonged, but they did not demand an exclusive embrace. One could belong to other groups as well.[45]

It is interesting that New Age religion and spirituality today is so thoroughly similar to the religions, mystery cults, and philosophies of the Hellenistic culture in which Christianity emerged. New Age religion and spirituality does not have a common set of beliefs and therefore does not require conversion to belief. Neither does it have a common ethical standard to which a person is required to conform. Nor does New Age spirituality have a distinct body of people to which a person belongs.[46]

These three aspects of the Christian faith—believing, behaving, and belonging—constitute the countercultural nature of the Christian faith. The early church preached these three unique characteristics of Christian conversion in the ancient Roman and Hellenistic world. Pagan religion made no demand on what a person believed or how they behaved, and pagans had no community to which they belonged. So it is today. The church ministers in a secular society characterized by the widespread influence of a relativistic spirituality that makes no demands and offers no real hope. To be effective in today's world, the church must refrain from accommodation to the easy believism of the post-Christian culture and call people into a conversion that reshapes the way they think and live. The church must also provide a community of genuine relationships and support in which new Christians can grow.

Conclusion

In this chapter I have focused on how people are converted in a post-Christian world. Postmodernity is at once secular because it rejects the God of Scripture yet at the same time religious because it invites people into a relativistic spirituality that makes no demands in terms of what is believed or how one behaves. Drawing from the early church and its effective evangelism in a secular/spiritual world, we have learned the following approach to evangelism in our post-Christian world:

1. A relationship is established between a Christian and a non-Christian.
2. The interested non-Christian is invited to attend a neighborhood community fellowship where Christians gather to eat, socialize, and discuss spiritual issues.
3. The interested person is brought to the church where the gospel is embodied in community and rehearsed in worship.
4. Genuine conversion is characterized by believing, behaving, and belonging.
5. Conversion is a start, not an end.

To enable a local church to begin the process of evangelism through social networking, a resource has been created to make connection with non-Christians. *Follow Me!* is a sixty-page booklet containing stories from the Gospel of John along with questions for discussion and prayers to express the journey toward faith.[47] The content includes the identity of Jesus in John 1, stories of Nicodemus and the woman at the well, stories of miracles, the account of Jesus' death and resurrection, and an invitation to be a follower of Jesus. It is intended to provoke one-on-one discussion between a spiritual mentor and a seeker or in a small group.

Here is how this resource may be used. A person committed to evangelism will give the booklet *Follow Me!* to a friend, suggesting they meet over coffee or breakfast or in some other setting to discuss, "Who is Jesus, anyway?" Today there is a great deal of interest in pursuing this question, particularly in a nonthreatening situation. Each week, or however frequently the two agree to get together, they meet and walk through the stories from the Gospel of John at a pace that works for them. The mentor does not need to be able to answer all the person's questions from the texts. The primary value of *Follow Me!* is that it provides an opportunity to discuss the faith based on the life, ministry, and work of Jesus Christ. The next step is to bring the person to church when he or she is ready to meet the Christian community and experience truth embodied in the hospitality of God's people, moving worship, challenging sermons, and the lifestyle of Christians. *In this context faith will be birthed.* Genuine repentance *(metanoia)*, a turning from sin and a turning to Jesus Christ as personal Savior and Lord of life, occurs through an immersion in embodied truth.

EMBODIED TRUTH

After a person becomes a Christian, he or she next begins the trajectory of discipleship formation. This second stage is a more intense period of experiencing and learning the believing, behaving, and belonging aspects of the faith.

Once a person has been converted, the church needs to provide a *rite of passage*. This passage rite will clearly indicate repentance of sin, a renunciation of evil, a transition to faith in Jesus Christ, and a commitment to becoming a disciple and living a transformed life. Each congregation must decide which passage rite to use that best moves the convert into the next phase of the process—discipleship. There are three passage rites that express this transition, each with its own nuances. They are:

the rite of baptism
the rite of conversion
the rite of welcome

For an explanation of these rites and their use, see appendixes 1 and 2.

Table 9: Evangelism Occurs within Community

Theme	Comments
Secular/spiritual seeker	A new kind of seeker has emerged in the post-Christian world. This seeker is shaped by the secular world and its values but longs for spiritual fulfillment.

Theme	Comments
Reach out through social networking	Early Christians, living in a culture similar to ours, reached out by being open to others and creating a welcoming community. Today social networking is the primary way of reaching out. Establish one-on-one relationships and neighborhood groups for social and spiritual community.
Build community	The epistemological shift is from evidence that demands a verdict to communication through an immersion in a community of embodied faith. Priority is given to relationship—eating together and meeting in neighborhood groups. Faith is on display. Worship proclaims and enacts truth. The witness of the Spirit is key.
The nature of conversion	Believing Behaving Belonging

Questions for Discussion

1. Is your church prepared to be a witness in the post-Christian world? How?
2. Does your church engage the secular seeker or the secular/spiritual seeker? Both? How?
3. Rate your church on the following:
   - open and accessible to others
   - adheres to an exclusive message
   - has created a sense of community
4. Do you reach out into the broader social network of the church
   - through neighborhood groups?
   - in believers' homes?
   - by eating together?
5. Do you take a post-Christian approach to evangelism? Evaluate:
   - Do we embody the faith in our community?
   - Are new converts immersed in the reality of the community?
6. Do you practice worship evangelism through worship that tells and enacts truth? Explain.
7. Evaluate your conversion expectations in terms of:
   - believing
   - behaving
   - belonging
8. Do you practice a post-Christian sequence of belonging, then behaving, then believing?
9. Would you find *Follow Me!* to be a helpful resource?

4

DISCIPLESHIP

The major concern of the International Consultation on Discipleship is the failure of the church to disciple new converts. This issue is experienced within the broad scope of the evangelical church. For example, Bill Hull in *The Disciple-Making Pastor* charges that "the Great Commission has been worshiped, but not obeyed. *The church has tried to get world evangelization without disciple making.*"[1] Michael Wilkins reports that in a class on the theology of disciple making he begins by asking, "Has anyone ever discipled you?" "The most common answer," he says, "is no!"[2] What Hull and Wilkins affirm in their pastorates, the International Consultation points to as a major problem throughout the evangelical world. We evangelicals have been concerned to fill our churches with new converts, but many of us have neglected the task of discipleship.

Discipleship is a lifelong process, and the church must attend to keeping and forming disciples throughout life. This chapter speaks to *initial* discipleship. How does the church introduce the new Christian to his or her calling to grow and mature as a disciple of Jesus? To approach this question we first ask, What does it mean to become a disciple?

The Nature of Discipleship

The nature of Christian discipleship is first revealed in the relationship Jesus sustained with the Twelve. In the sending out of the twelve disciples, Jesus said, "A student is not above his teacher, nor a servant above his master. It is enough for the student to be like his teacher, and the servant like his master" (Matt. 10:24–25). The first commitment of discipleship is to be a disciple of Jesus only!

This was a new concept in the world of Jewish rabbis. Prior to Jesus, the goal of a person being discipled was to exceed the master and gain his own following. For example, in Israel there were many rabbis with a following of disciples. A new disciple would sign on under a teacher with the hope that someday he would become a teacher and gain his own following of people. In a world of competitive rabbis, the learner hoped to outdo his teacher and become renowned as a teacher and leader so that people would study under him.

The first-century situation was much like the relationship between students and teachers today. On every campus we have the "renown teacher," and in churches we have "renown pastors." These teachers and pastors enjoy a following of disciples. Denominations are built around great teachers such as Luther, Calvin, Menno, or Wesley. While schools of thought are built around each of these great leaders, none of them has exceeded Jesus. In fact, in their writings and leadership they always point beyond themselves to lead people to be like Jesus, the one true teacher.

The concept of discipleship Jesus introduced ran counter to the prevailing notion of the teacher-disciple relationship. Jesus was not making disciples who would learn of him, become independent of him, and then make disciples of their own. His goal was that his disciples would make disciples not of themselves but that they would go forth to make disciples of Jesus. There are at least six ways Jesus taught his disciples to make disciples of himself:

1. They are to deliver the same message: "Repent, for the kingdom of heaven is near" (Matt. 4:17).
2. They are to exercise his compassion: "When he saw the crowds, he had compassion on them, because they were harassed and helpless, like sheep without a shepherd" (Matt. 9:36).
3. They are to follow the same religious and social traditions of Jesus (Matt. 12:1–8). "Look! Your disciples are doing what is unlawful on the Sabbath" (v. 2).
4. The disciples all belong to the same family of obedience (Matt. 12:46–50). "Whoever does the will of my Father in heaven is my brother and sister and mother" (v. 50).
5. The disciples are to emulate the servanthood attitude of Jesus (Matt. 20:24–28). "Whoever wants to become great among you must be your servant . . . just as the Son of Man did not come to be served, but to serve, and to give his life as a ransom for many" (vv. 26–28).

6. Jesus' disciples share in his destiny of suffering (Matt. 10:16–25). "On my account you will be brought before governors and kings. . . . When they arrest you, do not worry" (vv. 18–19).[3]

One who becomes a disciple of Jesus does not become a disciple in order to surpass Jesus and disciple people in his or her own name. Paul is an example of a disciple who did not call people to be disciples of himself but to be disciples of Jesus. However, there is a school of thought that sees Paul as a rival to Jesus. I met a man of this persuasion on a recent trip to the West Coast. On the airplane I sat next to an intelligent and well-trained rabbi. "You know," he said, "if it hadn't been for Paul, you and I would be in the same faith." "What do you mean?" I asked. "You Christians," he said, "are not followers of Jesus, you follow Paul." Immediately I saw that this rabbi thought of Paul as a teacher in competition with Jesus and not really a disciple of Jesus. He went on, "Paul, you know, completely reinterpreted Jesus. He turned Jesus into a metaphysical being, made him one with the Father, developed the idea of his death as an atonement for sin, argued for his resurrection and second coming, and ended up turning Jesus into something he was not. Jesus was a rabbi, teaching people how to live, but Paul turned him into a Savior and Redeemer, and you Christians have followed Paul, not Jesus. We Jews affirm Jesus' teachings but not Paul's interpretation of Jesus. So, if it wasn't for Paul, Jews and you followers of Jesus would be one religion." His comments made for a very interesting conversation.

Christians don't understand Paul to be in competition with Jesus. Paul's mission was to bring people to Jesus, to disciple them in Jesus' name. When Paul was in prison he wrote to the church at Philippi asking for their prayers that God would give him "sufficient courage so that now as always Christ will be exalted in my body, whether by life or by death. For to me, to live is Christ and to die is gain" (Phil. 1:20–21).

True discipleship is to follow after Jesus and no one else. The work of the church in its initial discipleship is to make this concept of discipleship clear to the new disciple. "We are not making you a disciple of this church, this pastor, this denominational preference, or this or that theological teacher. We are first and foremost making you a disciple *of Jesus.*"

How Does One Become a Disciple?

The three aspects of discipleship that stand out in the New Testament and early Christian era is that discipleship entails believing, belonging, and behaving. To follow Jesus and be his disciple one must believe what the Bible teaches about him: "But these are written that you may believe that Jesus is the Christ, the Son of God, and that by believing you may have life in his name" (John 20:31). A disciple must belong to the community of believers: "They devoted themselves to the apostles' teaching and to the fellowship, to the breaking of the bread and to prayer. . . . And the Lord added to their number daily those who were being saved" (Acts 2:42, 47). A disciple is also called to a new life of ethical behavior: "Do not conform any longer to the pattern of this world, but be transformed by the renewing of your mind" (Rom. 12:2). The process of initial discipleship practiced by the early church and advocated by this book is a process that initiates a new disciple into the lifelong commitment to grow in the knowledge and understanding of the faith, to take on a full, conscious, and active life in the church, and to commit to a new way of life. These three aspects of discipleship do not always happen sequentially. They are circles of growth and commitment that span a lifetime.

How the Church Disciples

I have already commented on how the church is the new apologetic in the post-Christian era. In the modern world people were attracted to an idea. Consequently, much of the apologetic of the modern world emphasized the reasonableness of the Christian faith and appealed to evidences of God, the coherence of the Bible, and the logic of believing in God. In our postmodern world, however, people are not nearly as interested in rational arguments. They want to see truth embodied and made real. Consequently, the church as a genuine community of God's people is the context not only for evangelism but also for lifelong discipleship.

The new disciple, then, who may have come to initial faith in Jesus through his or her association with the church has now, since conversion, come into an owned relationship with Christ and his church. The passage rite (of baptism, conversion, or welcome) has indicated a new kind of belonging in the church. This means that the church must consider how belonging to the church in this initial stage of discipleship actually disciples a new Christian into a deeper understanding of the faith and a greater commitment to the Christian lifestyle. What does the church do to disciple new Christians?

In the early church new disciples were formed by the nature of the church itself and by its worship and preaching. New Christians were also mentored in small groups and in one-on-one relationships. We look at how disciples may be formed today using the same methods of the early church.

Formed through Immersion into the Life of the Church

How does the church actually form and mold Christians? We begin, not with what the church does, but with what the church is.

As previously pointed out, the church is the witness to the reality of God's activity in history. The church is a witness to the entire story of God. It witnesses to the triune nature of God, to God as Creator, to God's involvement in history, to God's incarnation in Jesus Christ, to his sacrificial death, resurrection, and victory over the powers of evil, to his ascension and rule over all things, and to his coming again to restore creation in the new heavens and the new earth.

Yet this witness of the church is not in words alone. The church not only *says* God's mission, it *does* God's mission because it embodies the very reality of God. The church by its very existence makes the reality of God present. For example:

The church's experience of community reflects the eternal relationship of Father, Son, and Spirit.

The church's love of creation is an embrace of God's manifest creativity.

The church's central focus on Jesus affirms it as a continuous witness to the presence of Jesus.

The experience within the church of love, redemption, reconciliation, and peace is all a reflection of the redeeming work of Jesus.

The way of following Jesus, dealing with evil, and caring for the poor and needy are all signs of discipleship.

The hope and confidence in the future are expressions of the eschatological conviction of the faith.

Because the church is the reality of God made present, the church itself is a womb for disciple making. How the members of the church behave with each other and toward new disciples makes a lasting impact. It is, as the International Consultation on Discipleship states, "the primary community within which discipleship should take place."[4]

That the church is the context for discipleship is implied in Acts 2. Immediately after the story of Pentecost and the conversion and baptism of the first Christians, Luke launches into a description of their involvement in the church. New disciples immediately experienced the characteristics of the church—worship, teaching, prayer, fellowship, miraculous signs, caring for the needy, and eating together (Acts 2:42–47). This very experience within the church is in itself disciple making. This is why Cyprian wrote, "You can not have God for your father if you have not the church for your mother."[5] Calvin, following Cyprian, wrote, "There is no other way of entrance into life, unless we are conceived by her, born of her, nourished at her breast and continually preserved under her care and government."[6] Wesleyan theologian Gregory Clapper sums up the role of the church in conversion and discipleship. It is, he says, "a call to join a converting *community*, a community that has chosen to take a hand in the Lord's work of joyfully renewing not just the church but all of creation."[7] The church is not a perfect society, but it is God's society. Here God's people are taking a journey together. The church witnesses to God's reality, to Christ's redeeming work, and to the Spirit's work of sanctification. The place to begin discipleship, then, is the church. The new disciple must be immersed in the life of the church because it is the presence of God's life in the world.

The concept of discipleship through immersion within the community draws not only from the biblical and historical understanding of how disciples are made, it also relates to how communication occurs in our postmodern world. Pierre Babin points to the difference of communication methods of today's culture with the modern era of communications. The modern world emphasized conceptual learning. Learning presupposed what Martin Buber called an I-IT, meaning an impersonal relationship. God and Christian truth was an object to believe in; the means of learning about God were primarily didactic. A person studied truth through reading and analysis of words and concepts. Conclusions were made on the basis of logic, evidence, and argument. While this kind of teaching is not totally rejected in the postmodern world, a new understanding of how learning takes place has emerged. It is learning through submersion in a culture.[8] We learn from our environment—from living in a particular family, going to a specific school, shopping at a mall, watching particular shows on television. For example, in today's world we are submerged in a culture of violence, sexual permissiveness, consumerism, and the like. This culture impacts us and shapes the way we view things and the way we live.

In the same manner the church communicates through an immersion into its reality. The church lives by a different vision and story. When a new disciple is submerged in the communal life of the church—in its story, its values, its perspective—the countercultural nature of the faith is caught and the disciple begins to be formed by immersion in the ways of the community.

Immersion into the community has the power to form disciples, but how? Consider how disciples are formed through worship, preaching, and mentoring.

Formed through Worship

Worship is not a program presented to an audience but an invitation to the congregation to participate in the story that sweeps from creation to re-creation. Through this context the church enables a new disciple to participate in the truth that worship rehearses and celebrates. There are three cycles of worship that enable a new disciple to participate in truth—daily worship, weekly worship, and yearly worship.

The early church taught the new disciple a form of daily prayer that enabled a person to experience the rhythm of the entire day from a Christian perspective. For example, Hippolytus instructed Christians to pray throughout the day—on rising for God's presence throughout the day, at nine in the morning remembering that Christ was nailed to the cross, at noon because of the darkness that fell over the earth, at three in the afternoon to mark the death of Jesus, at the time of sleep giving one's life over to God, and at midnight because all creation is at rest. Hippolytus taught that a full day of prayer reminds us "if ye thus act, and are mindful of these things, and teach them to one another, and cause the catechumens to be zealous, ye can neither be tempted nor can ye perish, since you have Christ always in your mind."[9]

What if a local church prepared a Scripture verse for these crucial moments of daily Christian remembrance? What if a church asked the whole congregation to pray these verses daily? What if the church taught new disciples to adopt this rhythm of daily prayer? What if the whole community actually did this? What kind of difference would it make in the prayer life of the whole community? How would this simple but profound experience of prayer impact the church?

Sunday worship marks weekly time from a Christian perspective. Every Sunday the story from creation to re-creation is the content of worship. In the early church Sunday was viewed as the eighth day. On day one God created the world. On day six, Saturday, God rested. On day seven, Jesus Christ rose from the dead and began the new act of creation. Sunday was not only the day to celebrate the resurrection, it was also the first day of the new creation, thus the eighth day—the day that remembered the first day of creation and the day of the beginning of the new creation. Weekly worship celebrates both creation and re-creation.

The early church also developed a yearly understanding of time, marking the entire year by the great saving acts of God:

Advent waits for the coming of the Messiah.

Christmas celebrates his arrival.

Epiphany heralds the message that Christ has come, not just for the Jews but for the Gentiles and for the whole world.

Lent marks the time to prepare for his death, a period that culminates in the rehearsal of God's saving deeds in history during Holy Week.

Easter is a fifty-day celebration of Christ's resurrection.

Pentecost celebrates the coming of the Holy Spirit, the inauguration of the church, and the message that Christ is King.

The season after Pentecost assures us of God's saving presence in the church as we anticipate the second coming.

This rhythm of time practiced by a congregation forms congregational discipleship and spirituality. Any new disciple immersed in this process is bound to be formed inwardly by these outward disciplines of worship.

Worship forms new disciples and the entire congregation into a community of praise and prayer when the worship is done with integrity and authenticity. Worship is an offering of praise and prayer; it is not entertainment, although it should be engaging and joyful. For example, I led a Saturday workshop at The Chapel, a large church in Akron, Ohio. On Sunday I was able to attend the worship of the church. I didn't know what to expect. What was the appeal of this church that drew more than ten thousand people on a Sunday? Was it entertainment worship? Was it flashy preaching? I was quite surprised to discover it was neither. It was integrity and authenticity. The worship leader, Jim Mitchell, stood before the huge congregation dressed in a suit, without a worship team, and without waving his arms or asking us to act excited. He simply led with his voice and with his head lifted upward as thousands of people sang from their hearts, following his lead. There was no show going on—it was song, prayer, Scripture reading, and sermon—all low-key but intense and authentic. In the middle of this huge church stood a twenty-foot cross with a purple cloth draped over the arms. (It was the season of Lent.) Before the sermon the pastor, Newt Larson, walked from the pulpit to the cross, and as he stood beneath the cross, he asked the entire congregation to turn and gaze on it. After a few moments of silence he said, "This is what it is all about," and then for about two minutes he talked in a moving way about the centrality of the cross. He then went to the pulpit and without any show or glitz opened his Bible and gave an exegetical sermon. I asked myself, "Why do so many people come to this church?" and I answered, "People are sick of show and superficial rah-rah Christianity. They want the real thing. They want a challenge to be real disciples and live the Christian life in an authentic way." The worship in this church did just that. Because of its integrity, it drew people into its reality and discipled them into an authentic faith.

What is going on in this kind of worship is an authentic dialog between God and God's people. There are two sides to worship: divine action and human response.[10] God's presence is made real in the gathering of the people, in the preaching of the Word, in the action of the symbols, and in the sending forth of the people. Their continued response to God is expressed in their participation. When worship is a program, people sit back and expect to be entertained. "Entertain me with good music; tell me some good jokes; inspire me with great illustrations!" This attitude is just the opposite of intentional and prayerful worship. When the people intend worship, they intend to gather in God's presence; they intentionally pray, sing, listen to the sermon, take bread and wine, and go forth to live as disciples of Jesus. Teaching new disciples to be intentional in the cycles of daily, weekly, and yearly worship has the power to form them into living embodiments of truth. Intentional worship intensifies the experience of faith; it forms the individual and the entire corporate body.

What is the result of this kind of worship? The first result is that something is learned about God. Participatory worship teaches and forms. To use an old word, it *catechizes*. It shapes the new disciple's perception of faith and invites the disciple to deepen his or her relationship with God. How? Good worship will use the *language of mystery* and thus experience what Rudolph Otto called the *mysterium tremendum*.[11] God's otherness is not merely spoken as a propositional statement to be casually repeated. Rather, the experience of the numinous results in an inability to speak—a speechlessness before the holiness and majesty of God. Good worship will also use the *language of story*. Story expresses the intelligible aspect of the faith—God's involvement in history, his battle with the powers, his victory over sin through the death and resurrection of Jesus, our responsibility to live under the rule of Christ, and our anticipation of the new heavens and earth. These truths become more clearly known in a language that is understandable and intelligent. Finally, there is the *language of symbol*, the language of the Spirit. Through the symbols of faith—the Bible, the bread and wine, the cross—the presence of God is made known, not as a mere intellectual idea, but as a present reality in the lives of God's people.

Worship in which the disciple learns that God is wholly other, involved in history, and present will allow the disciple to pass through a whole range of emotions that affect his or her "knowing." Experiences teach and form. They move people, change them, and transform their lives. In worship the experience of the numinous, of the story of God's redemption, and of God's presence are experiences that evoke the spiritual life. Canadian philosopher Donald Evans points to eight "attitude virtues" that can be formed through experience. Worship has the power to shape these attitudes in the new disciple:

1. Basic trust (opposite: basic distrust)
2. Humility (opposite: pride/self-humiliation)
3. Self-acceptance (opposite: self-rejection)
4. Responsibility (opposite: irresponsibility)
5. Self-commitment (opposite: alienated dissipation of self)
6. Friendliness (opposite: self-isolation)
7. Concern (opposite: self-indulgence)
8. Contemplation (opposite: and self-consciousness)[12]

The early church fathers understood the relationship between the experience of worship and a discipleship of faith and obedience. Cyril of Jerusalem "wants nothing else from us than a good intention or purpose. He understands 'intention' not as an idle moral wishing, but a decisive living out of the gospel way."[13] Good worship is a way of forming disciples through truth proclaimed and enacted.

Formed through Preaching

Another aspect of worship that carries significant weight in disciple making is preaching. Thom Rainer's research among growing churches points to preaching as the most decisive factor in choosing a church,[14] and it remains an especially important factor in discipleship.

The early church placed a great deal of emphasis on discipleship through preaching. The direct information we have about preaching from Hippolytus is scant. He writes, "Let the catechumens spend three years as hearers of the word. But if a man is zealous and perseveres well in the work, it is not the time but his character that is decisive."[15] From this and other sources we know that the new disciple was formed through preaching for several years before he or she moved on to the next stage of spiritual formation. We also know that new disciples were mentored, especially in small groups that met *after the sermon* while members remained for the Lord's Supper. In addition to the Sunday sermon and the discussions after the sermon, new Christians could also attend daily services of the Word. For example, in Caesarea in the church pastored by Origen there was a daily morning service that included (1) an opening prayer, (2) a Scripture reading, (3) a sermon, and (4) a formal blessing, prayers, and dismissal.[16] The service lasted about an hour and was primarily a time for teaching. It is possible that over the course of three years the entire Bible was covered (not every verse, but the whole story). While not every new disciple would attend all these daily teachings, the opportunities for Bible study and growth in the knowledge of the faith were certainly available.

Hippolytus also refers to "instructors" who led the teaching and discussions after the sermon. While we do not know exactly who these instructors were, we may infer that they were laypeople gifted with the ministry of teaching and forming disciples.

In the *Constitutiones Apostolorum* an interesting insight is given to the possible content of this period. It states:

> Let him, therefore, who is to be taught the truth in regard to piety be instructed before his baptism in the knowledge of the unbegotten God, in the understanding of His only-begotten Son, in the assured acknowledgment of the Holy Spirit. Let him learn the order of the several parts of the creation, the series of providence, the different dispensations of your laws. Let him be instructed why the world was made, and why man was appointed to be a citizen there; let him also know his own nature, of what sort it is; let him be taught how God punished the wicked with water and fire, and glorified the saints in every generation . . . and how God still took care of, and did not reject, mankind, but called them from their error and vanity to acknowledge the truth at various seasons, leading them from bondage and impiety to liberty and piety, from injustice to justice, from death eternal to everlasting life.[17]

This quote shows that preaching in the early church was content oriented and instructional.

Another insight into preaching for discipleship is found in the preaching of Augustine. William Harmless describes Augustine's basilica as his classroom. He states:

> The rhythms of education moved to the rhythm of the liturgy itself. Every gesture, every sign, every word mattered—whether ritual greetings, sitting-and-standing arrangements, the cross people "wore" on their foreheads, or the secrecy of what followed dismissal. All these, Augustine insisted, held some import for how one believed, felt, and acted. In this classroom, silence was rare; instead, the atmosphere was rowdy, emotionally charged, more like that of a sports arena than a modern church. It offered entertainment as well as instruction, theatrics as well as worship: its drama was salvation history; its script was the scriptures; and its actors included everyone.[18]

In preaching, the new disciples mixed with the baptized and with outsiders. They heard substantial sermons that were usually an hour long that were directed not only toward "changed minds but changed hearts and changed lives."[19] The purpose of the sermon was to hear "the faith and pattern of Christian life." Augustine's sermons were "a 'cross-weave' of doctrine and of moral admonition" and were given to both the new disciples and to the faithful Christians so that "catechumens were instructed" and the "faithful were roused from forgetfulness."[20] Augustine writes of his own preaching, "When I unpack the holy scriptures for you, it is as though I were breaking open bread for you. You who hunger, receive it. . . . What I deal out to you is not mine. What you eat, I eat. What you live on, I live on. We have in heaven a common storehouse, for from it comes the word of God."[21]

Augustine never preached from a written manuscript. "He prepared only by prayer and study."[22] While the congregation stood (there were no pews), Augustine sat in a chair "in close proximity" to the people. Augustine was always highly sensitive to his congregation and appealed to their feelings and responded to their emotions, "sweeping them up into his own feelings."[23] His emphasis was to instruct them in such a way that it moved their hearts. As he said, "There is no voice to reach the ears of God save the emotion of the heart."[24]

The congregation was so involved in his sermon that they "would applaud whenever they recognized a favorite scripture verse. They would even interrupt and shout out the remainder of a verse he had begun to quote." "Clearly," writes Harmless, "Augustine brought something to his preaching—a style, a flair, a passion—that made these sermons not monological preachments, but engaging dialogues."[25]

What Can We Learn from the Early Church for Today?

One aspect of the ancient time of discipleship that is probably not transferable for today is the length of it (two to three years). What I suggest for today's church is the development of an *initial* discipleship, which, like the early church, would regard worship and preaching as an important part of discipleship. Preaching would follow either the design of the lectionary or a pattern designed by the preacher or staff. In this setting the goal of preaching is to inspire a love of God's Word in the new disciple and in the congregation at large.

How does one preach in a post-Christian world so as to develop a love of Scripture and thus disciple new and older Christians into an obedience to God's Word?[26] The International Consultation on Discipleship puts preaching and discipleship together in its statement that "we commit ourselves to preaching the gospel and making disciples,"[27] but it gives no direction on what this kind of preaching looks like. We can take a few clues from the preaching of the early fathers.

The first principle of preaching from the early church applicable for today is that it should be Scripture based. In recent years some have taught that the best way to preach in today's world is to draw on themes that interest people—how to manage money, how to raise children, how to find meaning. Sermons like this frequently draw on pop psychology and incorporate verses or themes of the Bible to interest a person in Scripture. This approach to preaching is primarily intended to reach the secular mind. As previously indicated, however, the post-Christian mind is more in tune with spirituality and is interested in the sources of spiritual traditions. Consequently preaching into a post-Christian world and especially preaching to new disciples who have already made a commitment to Christ will best serve discipleship when it focuses on what the Bible says. What we learn from the church fathers is a more direct form of preaching the Scripture. This kind of preaching doesn't say, "Here is how the Bible may help you in your quest for meaning," as though the quest for meaning is an autonomous journey that every person takes and uses the wisdom of the Bible to reach the goal. Rather, preaching in a post-Christian situation needs to be more direct. It says, "You are a disciple of Jesus. This is what disciples believe. This is how disciples live. Put yourself under the Word of God and live in obedience to his teaching." It is "submission to the Word" preaching that disciples Christians, not preaching that says, "In your journey of faith take what you like and what seems helpful to you." This latter position is the opposite of discipleship. It makes the person the arbiter of truth. It says, "I will decide what is true for me from Scripture." This kind of preaching is doomed to failure because it puts the person in the position of deciding what is true on the basis of convenience or personal preference. Preaching that is based on Scripture says, "Scripture—all of it—is true. Put yourself under it and live in obedience to it!"

A second insight from the early church fathers for preaching in today's post-Christian world is that preaching needs to be related to the full Christian story. All Scripture relates to the great story from creation to incarnation, death and resurrection to re-creation. All Scripture needs to be understood and interpreted within this grand sweep of God's mission to the world. Christian discipleship is not a private journey of the soul but a public witness of God's grand design for the universe.

Preaching from the larger context of God's story brings us to a third lesson from the early church, namely, preaching the centrality of Christ. Augustine, for example, put Christ at the center of the story by emphasizing how Christ is the second Adam, the one who has come to rescue us from the plight created by the first Adam. "In *Enarratio* on Psalm 119, he contrasted the descent of Christ with the fall of Adam:

> because Adam fell
> Christ therefore descended:
> the first fell,
> the other descended;
> the first from pride,
> the other descended in mercy."[28]

When new disciples see that Christ is at the center of the story and that all Scripture ultimately points to him, it provides them with a new interest in reading the Scripture christologically. I have always read Psalm 1 as a design for my holy living: "Happy are those who do not follow the advice of the wicked, or take the path that sinners tread, or sit in the seat of scoffers" (v. 1 NRSV). The passage has always meant much to me, but when I discovered that the early church fathers interpreted this chapter as referring primarily to Jesus Christ, a new meaning leapt into view. Christ does for me what I cannot accomplish myself! This message of grace is a motivation to live a life that does not "walk" in the way of sin, not as a means to achieve grace, but as a thankful response to the grace that comes through Jesus, who as the second Adam did for me what I cannot do for myself.

Finally, the early church fathers call us to preach to the heart as well as to the mind. William Harmless points out that like other church fathers, Augustine "set up an unusual contrapuntal effect: in the sermons on the Psalms, he focused on educating the catechumens' *hearts*, encouraging a journey at once upward and inward; in the sermons on John, he focused on educating the catechumens' *minds*."[29] How do you preach to both heart and mind today? It will happen through the kind of preaching that evokes a love of Scripture and a desire to live under the text. In this way the Bible is not only the book we read but, as Hans-Ruedi Weber has taught us, "the book that reads me."[30]

Formed through Mentoring

Hippolytus does not give us a great deal of insight into how mentoring worked in the early church, but it does figure prominently in the formation of disciples in the early church. The first mention of the mentor is made in the inquiry stage when new converts are first brought to the church to become hearers of the Word or *new disciples.* Hippolytus writes, "They who bring them shall testify that they are competent to hear the words." "They who bring" refers to the persons who first witnessed to them through their social network. It appears from the text that the person being brought has already made an initial commitment to Jesus Christ. Their status as converts is suggested by a reference to them as "new converts of the faith, who are to be admitted as hearers of the word."[31] The mentor who brought the new convert to the church also stands with him or her at the passage rites and continues as mentor throughout the discipleship process.

This kind of mentoring relationship will also occur in the process of discipleship today. The believer who first witnessed to his or her friend may walk through the process of new discipleship, standing with the new disciple at the various passage rites and meeting with the new disciple for prayer and study on a weekly basis to discuss the discipleship resources.

What is mentoring? Robert Clinton, author of a number of books on mentoring, simply defines mentoring as "one person helping another person to grow."[32] The *how* of mentoring is defined by Henry Simon as "having something to share with another who needs it to help him grow."[33]

A church may want to initiate a class to help mentors learn how to mentor, because the benefits of having trained mentors in the congregation are enormous. Mentoring is not only the means of growing a church but the means through which a mentor and the new disciple will deepen their faith as they grow together. Mentoring not only makes disciples, it impacts the entire church in its journey of discipleship.

Hippolytus also refers to what we can call a "small group" process in the making of disciples. New disciples were dismissed after the sermon to go to another place in the church where they were instructed, prayed for, and dismissed.[34] (The faithful remained for the Eucharist.) We know very little about the exact content and form of this small group. Presumably it consisted of a discussion of the sermon and its implications and a time of prayer with a meaningful dismissal.

In modern times the small group experience of discipleship was pioneered by John Wesley in what became known as the "class meeting."[35] Wesley based the class meetings on his interpretation of what was happening in the early church. He wrote, "As soon as any of these [referring to new converts] was so convinced of the truth as to forsake sin and seek the gospel salvation, they immediately joined them together, and met those *kataxoumenoi* 'catechumens' (as they were called) apart from the great congregation that they might instruct, rebuke, exhort, and pray with them and for them, according to their inward necessities."[36]

Today's revival of Wesley's small group movement has become an effective means of discipleship. In the process presented in this book, a small group gathering plays a central role in making disciples. The particular group for this stage of the process would meet once a week during the time of initial discipleship to discuss the sermon and matters pertaining to initial discipleship, pray together, and provide mutual support through accountability.

Conclusion

In this chapter we have explored the matter of initial discipleship. What do you do with a new convert to begin the process of making a disciple? We have answered that question by suggesting we look at how the church as a corporate body disciples. We have explored how new Christians are discipled through an immersion in community, through participation in worship, through the formative power of preaching, and through personal mentoring and small group accountability.

A resource has been prepared for use in this initial time of discipleship. *Be My Disciple!*[37] is a sixty-page booklet that contains ten Scripture lessons to train initial disciples. It covers three very important issues—discipleship through belonging to the church, discipleship through learning to worship, and discipleship through learning how to pray the Scripture.

Here is how this resource may be used: A mentor and new disciple may meet for coffee in a one-on-one discipleship situation and walk through the ten Scripture studies one week at a time. The mentor does not need to have all the answers. His or her support and prayer will be central to the matter of the new disciple becoming acquainted with the sources of discipleship—the community, worship, and Scripture—and learning how to draw on these resources for the journey in discipleship. A second way of using the resource *Be My Disciple!* is to accomplish the same goals as does the one-on-one mentoring but through meeting in a small group of accountability.

One additional goal of either one-on-one mentoring or small group accountability is to ready the new disciple for the next rite of passage that transitions him or her into a time of initial spirituality. This rite of passage will vary from church to church depending on the sequence of passage rites they have chosen to follow, but one possibility is the rite of covenant (see appendixes 1 and 2).

Table 10: The Nature of Discipleship

Theme	Comments
What does it mean to become a disciple?	In the Hebrew past a disciple hoped to exceed his master and disciple his own followers. The disciples of Jesus did not seek followers of themselves. They sought to make disciples of Jesus. The first commitment of Christian discipleship is to be a disciple of Jesus only.
How does one become a disciple?	Believing Belonging Behaving These three aspects of discipleship constitute a circle and are not necessarily sequential. The circle continues in ever-increasing depth throughout all of life.

Table 11: How the Church Disciples

Theme	Comments
The church forms disciples through an immersion in its life.	Immersion into the life of the church, which is the body of Christ on earth, is disciple making as the new Christian is assimilated into the embodied reality of God's kingdom.
Worship forms disciples.	Worship says and does truth. Show me how you worship and I'll tell you what you believe and what kind of disciple you are becoming.
Preaching forms disciples.	Preaching sets forth the faith and pattern of Christian living.
Mentoring forms disciples.	One-on-one mentoring or small group accountability presses home the need for daily discipleship.

Questions for Discussion

1. What does your congregation currently do to disciple new Christians?
2. How does your congregation currently disciple new Christians in believing? belonging? behaving?
3. When a new Christian becomes immersed in your community, will that immersion form the new Christian to follow Jesus? Or does your church follow another leader? Or is your congregation so dysfunctional that immersion into the community will make it difficult to follow Jesus?
4. Does the worship of your congregation proclaim and enact the Christian story? Or is worship a program, maybe even a show?

5. Does the preaching of your church instruct new Christians into the faith and pattern of Christian living? Or is the preaching more along the lines of self-help?
6. How does your community mentor new Christians?
7. Could *Be My Disciple!* be of help to you?

SPIRITUAL FORMATION

The third step of Christian formation is to help the new Christian begin the spiritual life. While the spiritual life begins with conversion, the new Christian needs a time set aside to learn the pattern of spirituality. Taking time to learn what it means to be a spiritual person is suggested by the International Consultation on Discipleship, who recognize discipleship as a "process."[1] Not everything can be accomplished at once, yet in most of our churches the new Christian is plunged into everything at once. There is a need to recognize the stages of the process. Once the new Christian has been introduced to what it means to be a disciple, the next obvious step is to provide some initial training in what it means to be spiritual.

In a new book, pollster George Gallup Jr. cites the meteoric rise of interest in things spiritual. He quotes Christian commentator Martin Marty, who said that "spirituality is back almost with a vengeance." Concern for the spiritual, writes Gallup, is "out of the closet," but he warns, "all that passes for spirituality in our culture will not stand the test of time or authentic practice." Some of what is passed off as spirituality "does little more than make our eyes mist up or your heart warm."[2]

A Nebraska pastor, concerned about the state of current spirituality, wrote, "We are living in a secular society but a spiritual culture."[3] The spiritual culture is the widespread influence of New Age spirituality—a spirituality of the self. "The basic New Age claim is that what is wrong with the person and the world can only be dealt with properly by encountering and thereby unleashing that which lies 'within.' The New Age claims that 'self-spirituality' can make a difference to what it means to be human and fulfilled. This belief translates into practices of healing, work, relationships, community life, politics, sex—indeed, all areas of human experience."[4] The reality of New Age spirituality leads Gallup to conclude that "at the very time it grows in popularity, *spirituality* has become more and more an elusive term. More and more, one crying out for definition."[5]

Considering the widespread use of the word *spirituality*, new Christians need to be informed about *Christian* spirituality. What is it, and how does the church help new Christians form the spiritual life? These are two questions addressed in this chapter.

What Is Christian Spirituality?

A cursory glance at recent books on spirituality yields a confusing array of definitions. Most are couched in academic terminology and result in bewilderment. For example, one respected author defines spirituality as "the quest for fulfilled and authentic existence, involving the bringing together of the fundamental ideas of Christianity and the whole experience of living as the basis of and within the scope of the Christian faith."[6] This definition is far too cumbersome to put before a new disciple. The biblical definition of spirituality is more simple, yet more profound.

In the next few pages I will explore the teaching on spirituality found in Scripture, especially the writings of Paul. Paul's understanding of spirituality is simple and direct: spirituality is to live in the pattern of the death and resurrection of Jesus. Paul's signature statement on spirituality is in his discussion of baptism in Romans 6: "We were therefore buried with him through baptism into death in order that, just as Christ was raised from the dead through the glory of the Father, we too may live a new life" (v. 4). The true identity of the Christian is with Jesus Christ in his death and resurrection. True Christian spirituality is to live out our baptism by continually dying to sin and rising to the new life in Christ. The work of the church in forming the spiritual life of the new disciple is to *train the new Christian in the practice of living in the pattern of the death and resurrection of Jesus Christ*.

In order to grasp more clearly this Pauline understanding of spirituality, a view that dominated the early church and its way of forming the spiritual life, it needs to be put into the greater context of Paul's theology.

Spirituality in the Theology of Paul

First, the central theme of Paul's theology is the death and resurrection of Jesus.[7] Here is where Paul begins every conversation. For example, when some from Corinth doubted the resurrection of Jesus, Paul wrote that the message he had received and then proclaimed all over the Roman Empire was the Good News that "Christ died for our sins according to the Scriptures, that he was buried, that he was raised on the third day" (1 Cor. 15:3–4). He argued that nothing in the Christian faith is more central, more pivotal, than the death and resurrection. "If Christ has not been raised, your faith is futile" (1 Cor. 15:17).

Second, for Paul the death and resurrection of Jesus is the key to understanding the whole story that sweeps from creation to re-creation. Paul teaches that Jesus is the second Adam who has reversed the human situation. The first Adam, by his sin, plunged the whole human race into sin. Our relationship with God was broken because of Adam, but in Jesus the second Adam has appeared. In the incarnation God was made flesh. In the union between God and man, Jesus repeated the role of Adam. This time, however, through the life, death, and resurrection of Jesus Christ, the second Adam, the sin of the first Adam was reversed. "For since death came through a man, the resurrection of the dead comes also through a man. For as in Adam all die, so in Christ all will be made alive" (1 Cor. 15:21–22). This man Jesus, who is fully God and fully man, did for us what we are not able to do for ourselves. Through his death and resurrection he has reversed the human condition of alienation with God and reconciled us to God. This reconciliation is assured because his death is a sacrifice for sin, a victory over the powers of evil, and a demonstration of how to live.

Jesus is Lord. He now rules in heaven over his entire creation and will return at the end of history to destroy all evil. "For he must reign until he has put all his enemies under his feet. The last enemy to be destroyed is death" (1 Cor. 15:25–26).

In summary, the context for understanding Paul's theology is that it is centered in the death and resurrection of Jesus, which provide the key to understanding everything in life from creation to the re-creation. The death and resurrection affirms that Christ is Lord of history, the Ruler over all things, the King of heaven and earth.

Baptismal Spirituality

Paul sees spirituality as an intentional entering into the death and resurrection of Jesus. After explaining the universal scope of the death and resurrection of Jesus in Romans 5, he immediately launches into the believer's personal identification with the death and resurrection of Jesus in Romans 6. Spirituality is a real, actual, and lived experience of entering into the death and resurrection. Baptism is the sign that we have been plunged into his death and raised into the power of his resurrection. By being "in Christ" we are to live the baptized life. Consequently Paul applies past tenses to death and sin in Romans 6: "our old self was crucified with him" (v. 6), therefore "we should no longer be slaves to sin because anyone who has died has been freed from sin" (vv. 6–7). On the other hand, Paul applies future tenses to the resurrected life. Thus "we too may live a new life" (v.4), and because we died with Christ, "we believe we will also live with him" (v. 8).

This life of continually dying to sin and rising to our new life in Christ is not easy. Paul describes the struggle in Romans 7 and confesses, "When I want to do good, evil is right there with me" (v. 21). In Romans 8, however, he assures the Christian that "there is no condemnation for those who are in Christ Jesus" (v. 1). Even though the struggle with sin is still present in our lives, we have the Spirit. "The mind of sinful man is death, but the mind controlled by the Spirit is life and peace" (Rom. 8:6). The Christian who is in Jesus and is now dead to the power of sin is controlled by the Spirit (v. 9). By the Spirit it is possible "to put to death the misdeeds of the body" (v. 13) because "the Spirit helps us in our weakness" (v. 26).

To summarize, Christian spirituality derives from a recognition on my part that:

1. I cannot do anything that puts me in a right relationship with God.
2. Jesus, by his death and resurrection, restores my relationship with God.
3. Through repentance and faith I trust in Jesus as the One who makes a relationship with God possible.
4. In baptism I identify with the death and resurrection of Jesus and choose to live my life according to the pattern of death and resurrection, continually dying to sin and rising to the new life in Jesus Christ.
5. I receive the seal of the Spirit, which signifies that my new life is to be lived by the power of the Spirit.

One way to describe the spirituality of Paul is to call it "baptismal spirituality." We are called to live in our baptism. In our identity with the death and resurrection of Jesus, we live a life empowered by the

Holy Spirit, a life that continually dies to sin and continually rises to the life of the Spirit.

A good case in point is the Galatian community of the first century. In Paul's letter to them he reviews what it means to be spiritual. He reminds them that they had heard the gospel and had begun to live in the Spirit, dying to the old man of sin and living in the freedom of the Spirit. However, some false prophets came into their midst and persuaded them that spirituality was earned. Those false teachers brought them under the law again. Paul addresses the Galatian embrace of self-attained spirituality head on. He passionately pleads with them not to be "burdened again with the yoke of slavery" (Gal. 5:1) and goes so far as to say that if they seek to be justified by the law they will be "alienated from Christ" and will have "fallen away from grace" (Gal. 5:4).

The solution Paul offers to the Galatian people is right in line with the precepts of spirituality laid down above. He admonishes them: "Those who belong to Christ Jesus have crucified the sinful nature with its passions and desires. Since we live by the Spirit, let us keep in step with the Spirit" (Gal. 5:24–25).

The spiritual life is to recognize that our spirituality is Jesus Christ. Therefore we are "called to be free" (Gal. 5:13). This freedom is to "live by the Spirit, and you will not gratify the desires of the sinful nature" (Gal. 5:16). The prescription Paul lays out for them to live in the Spirit is a recognition of spiritual warfare. The Christian life, which is rooted in Jesus' death and resurrection, follows the baptismal pattern of dying to sin and rising to new life in Christ. The spiritual person, living by the Spirit, puts off "the sinful nature . . . sexual immorality, impurity and debauchery; idolatry and witchcraft; hatred, discord, jealousy, fits of rage, selfish ambition, dissensions, factions and envy; drunkenness, orgies, and the like" (Gal. 5:19–21). Here Paul has described the normal Roman way of life. He is saying, "Christians have been baptized into a death to this kind of living." In contrast he sets forth the life of the Spirit: "The fruit of the Spirit is love, joy, peace, patience, kindness, goodness, faithfulness, gentleness and self-control" (Gal. 5:22–23). Christians have been baptized into the resurrected life, the life of the Spirit. They are to cultivate the habits of the Spirit because they have been identified with Jesus through repentance, faith, baptism, and the seal of the Spirit.

Spirituality among the Early Church Fathers

We have seen that Pauline spirituality stressed an identification with the death and resurrection of Jesus—an identification that resulted in the pattern of dying to sin and rising to the new life. But was this taught in the early church?

We turn now to review the teaching of the early church on spirituality—a teaching that prepares disciples to live in the pattern of dying to sin and rising to a life empowered by the Spirit. In early Christian teaching spirituality was not an earned state of being; instead, it was seen as a gift that came through Jesus and was signified by baptism. The spiritual life of putting off and putting on dominated the early church period and was taught with great intensity in the third stage of disciple making. I turn to a few of the frequent early church writings on this topic to demonstrate the importance of understanding the spiritual life as one that puts off evil and embraces the life of the Spirit.[8]

The *Didache*, which some date as early as 50 A.D., presents the two ways. For example, "Two ways there are, one of life and one of death, and there is a great difference between the two ways." "My child shun evil of any kind and everything resembling it. . . . On the contrary be gentle for the gentle will inherit the land." "Do not hesitate to give, and do not give in a grumbling mood . . . do not turn away from the needy; rather share everything with your brother."[9]

The following quote from the *Letter of Clement*, written around 96 A.D., points to the spiritual life centered in the work of Jesus and the call to live in the works of the Spirit: "So, we too, who have been called by his will in Christ Jesus, are sanctified not through ourselves, or through our wisdom or understanding or piety, or any works we perform in holiness of heart, but in the faith through which almighty God has sanctified all men from the beginning of time. . . . What then are we to do, brethren? Shall we rest from doing good, and give up love? May the master never permit that this should happen, at least not to us; but let us be eager to perform every good work with assiduity and readiness."[10]

While there are numerous illustrations of the two ways in the early church fathers, one more will suffice to give us an insight into the early church's grasp of spirituality. This quote from Irenaeus shows how Christ is the Victor over the powers of evil and how Christians are to live in this truth:

> So the word was made flesh that, through that very flesh which sin had ruled and dominated, sin should lose its force, and be no longer in us. Therefore the cross took that same original formulation with his entry into our flesh, so that he might come near and do battle on behalf of the fathers, and conquer by Adam that through Adam had stricken us down. . . .
>
> For the road of those who see is a single upward path, lighted by heavenly light; but the ways of those who see not, are many and dark and divergent. The former road heads to the kingdom of heaven by uniting

man with God; but the others bring man down to death by severing him from God.[11]

This teaching reflects Paul's emphasis on faith, baptism, and the Christian life. New Christians who have put on Christ are to be baptized and to adopt a way of life that turns away from evil and lives the life of the Spirit. We turn now to look more closely at how the content of spirituality may be taught to new Christians in our churches today.

Training New Christians to Be Spiritual Today

How we train new Christians to live out the pattern of the death and resurrection today is the concern of this third period of training. We may draw from the early church to learn how they taught spirituality through the image of baptism, through preaching, through a special time of prayer over the new Christians, through small groups and one-on-one discussion. These are safe contexts for learning the power of the baptismal image for the new life that is found through an identification with the death and resurrection of Jesus.

Teaching Spirituality through the Image of Baptism

The early church fathers frequently taught spirituality through the image of baptism. Cyril of Jerusalem, for example, in his *Catechetical Lectures* tells those who will soon be baptized, "When you go down into the water and are, in a fashion, entombed in the water as he was in the rock, you may rise again to walk in newness of life."[12] The instruction given by Cyril is clearly a reflection of Romans 6:11, "Count yourselves dead to sin but alive to God in Christ Jesus." In order to understand how the image of baptism can be used to train new Christians in spirituality, I will summarize the high points of baptism and what is learned from this rite as it was practiced in the early church.

The symbols that surround baptism speak to the Pauline understanding. Baptism was not taken lightly. First, only those who had demonstrated their conversion to Jesus as valid entered into a time of preparation for baptism. Hippolytus writes that their lives were examined "whether they have lived soberly, whether they have honored the widows, whether they have visited the sick, whether they have been active in well-doing."[13] The early church leaders recognized that it takes time to wean pagans from their amoral and narcissistic lives. How have they responded to the training? Have they chosen to live the Christian life? If not, they are not ready to be baptized. The church is not going to recognize a person who shows no aptitude for discipleship. If a person claims to be a convert but has not followed the teaching of Jesus and lived a new life, that person, writes Hippolytus, "shall be put aside as not having heard the word in faith; for it is never possible for the alien to be concealed."[14]

Those who are accepted for baptism pass through a series of symbols that bespeak their spiritual commitment of putting off sin, putting on Christ, and living by the Spirit. They have already demonstrated in their lives that they live as people of Jesus and the Spirit. Now they are to receive the outward symbols that affirm their Christian commitment and bring them into the full life of the church. Before baptism they attend an all-night service where they listen to Scripture readings that present God's creation, the fall, God's involvement in history from Abraham through Israel and the prophets, and finally God's incarnation in Jesus Christ to redeem the world.[15] Having been reminded of how God saved them and the world in Jesus Christ, they then go through the passage rite of baptism with all its symbols of how Jesus Christ rescued the world from the powers of evil. These symbols also speak to how their commitment to die to sin and be raised to the new life in Christ is symbolized in baptism.

For example, on Saturday morning Hippolytus instructs the bishop to do the following: "And, laying his hand on them, he shall exorcize all evil spirits to flee away and never to return; when he has done this he shall breathe in their faces, seal their foreheads, ears and noses, and then raise them up" (they have been on their knees). Next, as the candidate is standing in the baptismal waters, they are commanded to renounce Satan saying, "I renounce thee Satan, and all thy servants and all thy works." After the renunciation the presbyter is to anoint those who will soon be baptized with oil and say, "Let all spirits depart from thee."[16] After the baptism the newly baptized is again anointed with oil as a symbol of receiving the Holy Spirit. All these baptismal symbols are very clear. Baptism is the sign of (1) identity with Jesus, (2) dying to sin and being raised to the new life, and (3) the call to live a life in the Spirit.

The average evangelical church may choose not to adopt all the symbols used by the early church in baptism. However, I urge evangelical leaders to use at least one prominent symbol—the renunciation of evil. I was reared in a Baptist church, and when I was baptized at age twelve I was asked to renounce Satan. Standing in the waters of baptism, the pastor said to me, "Robert, do you renounce the devil and all his works?" I said, "I do," and years later I still remember this vow and continue to call on the Spirit to help me renounce evil and affirm the resurrected life. Most evangelical churches will do more than adopt this one symbol, but even if a church adopts just this one symbol, it will help the new believer and the entire church remember their call to live out the pattern of death and resurrection.

Teaching Spirituality through Preaching

In the early church it was the general custom to preach to the newly baptized on the full meaning of baptism *after* the new Christians were baptized. By preaching after baptism they were following the idea that experience precedes understanding. Today, if an evangelical church baptizes new Christians immediately after conversion, the same general practice of the early church will be observed. However, if baptism is delayed, preaching on baptism will occur before baptism. In most evangelical congregations, worship will draw a mixture of baptized and unbaptized people. Consequently, the preacher will need to apply baptismal preaching to both the baptized and the unbaptized.

Much has been written recently on the preaching of the early church fathers.[17] Their sermons are a gold mine of examples. We turn now to their sermons to understand how preaching today may teach that spirituality arises from the experience of being baptized into the death and resurrection of Christ and the importance of living in the pattern of dying and rising by the power of the Spirit.

I have already illustrated the warfare theme from the second and third centuries, so I will turn to the preaching of the fourth century that is directed toward those who are about to be baptized or those who have already been baptized. In these sermons we find once again that the theme of *Christus Victor* lies at the heart of spirituality. We begin with a quote from Gustav Aulén in his classic work, *Christus Victor*. Aulén's study of this theme in the literature and sermons of the early church leads him to conclude that spirituality in the classical Christian tradition cannot be understood apart from the theme of Christ's victory over the powers of evil—a victory he won as a result of the sacrifice of himself for sin. "The work of Christ is the overcoming of death *and sin;* strictly, it is a victory over death because it is a victory over sin. And, further, the note of triumph which rings through this Greek theology depends not only on the fact that his victory is the starting point for his present work in the world of men, where He, through His spirit, even triumphantly continues to break down sin's power and 'deifies' men."[18]

The church fathers root spiritual growth in the *Christus Victor* theme. Since Jesus Christ has overcome sin and death by his death and resurrection, so the believer who identifies with his death and resurrection through faith signified by baptism is to live a life of victory in his or her continuing struggle with sin. In this way, Aulén points out, the new Christian is "deified." This term, foreign to the language of evangelicals, means "united with God, brought closer to God" and is used essentially the same way as *sanctification,* a word common to the vocabulary of the reformers and to historic evangelicalism.

Space allows only one illustration of a *Christus Victor* spirituality from the fourth century. I turn to the catechetical lectures of Saint John Chrysostom, the bishop of Constantinople. The particular sermons from which I will draw were given in Antioch between 386 and 398 A.D., just before he went to Constantinople. Scholarship places these sermons during Lent of 388.[19] Therefore they were given *before* baptism, but they were also heard by those who had been baptized and served for them as a reminder of their baptismal spirituality. For those who were to be baptized, the sermon taught them the meaning of their baptism. I will only draw examples that touch on the explicit theme of baptism and the implications baptism holds for spirituality.

First, in his *second instruction* (there are twelve altogether), Chrysostom defines baptism: "Baptism is a burial and resurrection. For the old man is buried with his sin and the new man is resurrected, *being renewed according to the image of his creator.* We put off the old garment, which has been made filthy with the abundance of our sins; we put on the new one, which is free from every stain. What am I saying? We put on Christ Himself. For *all you* says St. Paul, who have been baptized into Christ, have put on Christ."[20]

Second, throughout his instructions Chrysostom connects baptism with the new birth. Some have questioned whether Chrysostom and other fathers taught baptismal regeneration—that baptism itself saves a person without the necessity of faith. Baptismal regeneration is a medieval view that has been associated with Roman Catholic theology, but it is certainly not an early church view. The early church fathers always presuppose that those who come to baptism already have faith, but they make much of the passage rite of baptism as the sign of that faith. In this emphasis they follow the teaching of Paul in Romans 6.

It is fashionable among some evangelical churches to downgrade and even neglect baptism in favor of decisional faith. The early church fathers associated faith and baptism together, but they placed a greater emphasis on the passage rite than do most evangelicals. The most appropriate analogy perhaps is that of engagement and marriage. While the ceremony affirms the love and commitment of the couple being married, it also confers upon that couple new rights and responsibilities. In the same way baptism confirms the faith already expressed (a prebaptized person is a convert and disciple) baptism symbolizes the new relationship with God and calls the newly baptized into a new life of living out his or her baptism. As an example from my own experience, I already had faith *before* I was baptized, but baptism was a powerful experience for me—especially the renunciation of Satan and all the powers of evil. To this day, when I am asked to give my conversion testimony, I always go back to my baptism.

Saint John Chrysostom, in his *fourth instruction*, preaches that faith in Christ and baptism makes one a new creation. He comments on Paul's statement that "everything old has passed away; see, everything has become new!" (2 Cor. 5:17 NRSV): "By this he showed in brief that those who, by their faith in Christ, had put off like an old cloak the burden of their sins, those who had been set free from their error and been illumined by the light of justification, had put on this new and shining cloak, this royal robe."[21]

In the same sermon Chrysostom immediately shows how an identification with Christ through faith and baptism is related to the spiritual life. Commenting on Paul's statement that "those who belong to Christ Jesus have crucified the flesh with its passions and desires" (Gal. 5:24 NRSV), he said, "Those who have dedicated themselves to Christ have nailed themselves to Him by this dedication and have jeered at the concupiscence of the body, just as if they had crucified themselves together with their passions and desires."[22]

It is faith in Christ and a baptism into his death and resurrection that images the meaning of spirituality. Because a person trusts in Christ and has signified this faith through baptism, his calling in faith and baptism is to live a life in the face of evil that always shines with the light of baptism. "See to it that you keep the garment in the same shining beauty. For as long as that wicked demon, the enemy of our salvation, sees this spiritual robe of ours all shining, he will not dare to stand near, because he is so afraid of its brightness. For the luster it sends forth blinds his eyes."[23]

Chrysostom launches forth to teach how faith and baptism call us to a new life. Space does not permit the development of these themes; let it suffice to say that Chrysostom throughout the twelve instructions draws primarily from the practical teaching of Paul and calls forth a spiritual life that is in keeping with the admonitions of the Epistles.

In *Creative Preaching on the Sacraments*, Craig Satterlee and Lester Ruth implore preachers to draw on the creative insights and imagistic preaching of the church fathers. They point to the preaching of the early church fathers as a model for preaching today. The fathers of the church compare the stories of the Old Testament to the actions of Jesus and the sacred actions of the church in baptism. Satterlee and Ruth write: "For example, the spirit moving over the waters at creation, God's presence with Noah and his family in the flood, Israel's crossing of the Red Sea, and the Holy Spirit descending on Jesus in the Jordan River all point to God's saving activity in baptism, where we die with Christ and are raised with him."[24]

They remind us that the hermeneutical key of the early church fathers is clearly the key to preaching in a post-Christian world. The "historical-critical method has distanced the church from its scriptures by making the Bible unintelligible to anyone who is not a trained expert in the history, language, culture and beliefs of the centuries and people spanned by the Bible."[25] On the other hand, the typological manner of the early church fathers is simple and communicates the meaning of Scripture in language and images that reach the common person. The key is this: "Interpret scripture according to its application to Christian life, and interpret the life of the Christian by its correspondence to scripture."[26]

In summary, the spiritual life is rooted in our identification with the death and resurrection of Jesus, and the call to live in the pattern of death to the old and a resurrection to the new must be preached. Preaching should call people to live in their baptism. Here is an image that will catch the imagination of postmodern people and sow a seed that will take a lifetime to harvest.

Teaching Spirituality through Prayer

During the third stage of Christian formation, the early church prayed specific prayers for the putting off of the old and the putting on of the new as the new converts prepared for baptism. Hippolytus refers to those prayers: "Hands shall be laid upon them daily in exorcism and, as the day of their baptism draws near, the bishop himself shall exorcize each one of them that he may be personally assured of their purity."[27]

In the third century these prayers were prayed during worship. The content of the prayer focused on the meaning of baptism and the spiritual life. They were prayers that called upon God to ready the person for baptism by helping him or her to put off temptation to evil and embrace the new life that is in Christ. Here is a sample of this prayer content: "Remember, you accursed devil, the sentence that was passed upon you, and give honor to the living and true God! Give honor to Jesus Christ his Son, and to the Holy Spirit, and depart from these servants of God whom our Lord Jesus Christ has called to receive His holy grace and blessing in the waters of baptism. We adjure you, cursed devil, never dare to violate it!"[28]

In today's world the image of calling forth those soon to be baptized or the recently baptized (depending on whether baptism is delayed or not) will have a powerful spiritual effect on those for whom the prayers are made and upon the entire congregation. Imagine doing these prayers for six consecutive Sundays. The pastor says, "Will those who are to be baptized [or those who have just been baptized] please come forward for prayer with their mentors." Here is the picture: Let's say six people step forward with their mentors; they kneel. The mentor stands behind and lays hands on the head of the one to be baptized. The pastor or someone else prays a well-thought-out prayer that deals with the combat with evil, calls upon the powers of evil to flee, and invokes the presence of the Spirit to empower these new Christians with the spiritual strength to live a new life. What kind of image does this create for the new Christian and for the entire congregation? It speaks loud and clear to the pastoral care of this congregation, of the communal commitment to live the new life, and of the meaning of the spiritual life.

Two Weapons of Warfare

During this third stage of Christian formation the new disciple is taught two weapons of warfare. How do you deal with the temptation of evil? The answer given by the early church is to memorize the Apostles' Creed and the Lord's Prayer and to repeat them both frequently as they become an inner armor of dependence upon God and a reminder of what the Christian believes. Augustine gave the following reason to the new Christians for learning the Apostles' Creed and the Lord's Prayer: "You have not first been taught the Lord's Prayer and then the creed. You have been taught the creed first, so that you may know what to believe, and afterwards the prayer, so that you may know whom to call upon. The creed contains what you are to believe; the prayer, what you are to ask for."[29]

William Harmless describes the importance of the Apostles' Creed and the Lord's Prayer: "The creed gave the 'what' of right belief, while the Our Father gave the 'to whom' and 'how' of right praise."[30] In this way right faith and right praise are brought together.

Think of the power of learning the Apostles' Creed and the Lord's Prayer in today's church. It was the custom in the early church for new Christians to say the Creed and the Lord's Prayer from memory. How significant would it be in today's church to ask the candidates for baptism or the newly baptized to stand before the congregation and repeat these great expressions of spirituality and weapons to be used in the daily struggle with evil?

Conclusion

In this chapter we have explored how new Christians may be introduced to the spiritual life. Spirituality has been defined as living in the pattern of the death and resurrection of Jesus Christ. We have visited that theme in the teaching of Paul and the early church fathers. We have seen how the theme of spirituality is imaged by baptism, and we have looked at how new Christians can have their eyes opened to their spiritual calling through embracing the image of baptism, preaching, prayer, and the internalization of the Apostles' Creed and the Lord's Prayer.

A special *resource* has been prepared to introduce new Christians to this ancient understanding of the spiritual life. This resource, *Walk in the Spirit!*, is a study of Scripture passages that deal with the Christian life through an understanding of Paul's theology of spirituality, through the power of prayer, and through the learning of the Apostles' Creed.[31] It is especially designed for use in a one-on-one relationship or in a small group study.

The rite of passage that will be used at the end of this period of Christian formation will vary from church to church, depending on the place of baptism. If baptism was the first rite of passage, used immediately after conversion, then the rite to use at this point in the Christian formation process is the *rite for the reaffirmation of baptism*. If baptism was delayed, the appropriate passage rite that ends this period of initial formation is the *rite of baptism*. (See appendixes 1 and 2 for suggestions on the content and use of these rites.)

Table 12: What Is Christian Spirituality?

Theme	Comments
The theology of Paul	True spirituality is a gift, not a state that is earned. Christ is our spirituality, which is established by God's grace through faith and trust in Jesus. God sees us through the righteousness of Christ.
Baptismal spirituality	Baptism is the image of our identification with Jesus. We are called to live in our baptism, continually dying to sin and continually rising to the new life in Christ. "Put off" the old, "put on" the new—this is the pattern of the spiritual life.
Spirituality among the early church fathers	There are two ways—one of death, the other of life. Choose life!

Table 13: Training New Christians to Be Spiritual Today

Theme	Comments
Teaching spirituality through the image of baptism	Recover the symbols of baptism: exorcism renunciation of Satan anointing with oil
Teaching spirituality through preaching	Recover the *Christus Victor* theme of the atonement
Teaching spirituality through prayer	Prior to baptism incorporate special prayers in worship for those who are about to be baptized. The content of prayer is that new Christians are to learn how to "put off" evil and "put on" Christ.
Two weapons of warfare	The Apostles' Creed: know what you believe. The Lord's Prayer: know on whom to call.

Questions for Discussion

1. What does your congregation currently do to form new Christians' spirituality?
2. Discuss this point: True spirituality is a gift, not a state that is earned.
3. Read Romans 6 and discuss this statement: We are called to live in our baptism, continually dying to sin and continually rising to the new life in Christ. The pattern of spirituality is the death and resurrection of Jesus.
4. How do the early church fathers confirm the theme of baptismal spirituality?
5. How can you employ the images of baptism to teach spirituality to your congregation?
6. How does the preaching of *Christus Victor* affirm baptismal spirituality?
7. Would you consider praying for baptismal candidates for several Sundays before baptism? What would you pray?
8. Would you consider teaching the Apostles' Creed and the Lord's Prayer to baptismal candidates as weapons of warfare? Would you also have them memorize these weapons and learn how to use them in the pattern of dying to sin and rising to new life?
9. Have you considered how *Walk in the Spirit!* may help you accomplish spirituality training?

6

CHRISTIAN VOCATION

What do you do to assimilate new Christians into the life of the church? How does Christian formation take place for those who are now in the church, baptized, discipled, and spiritually formed in an initial way? Our clue to this continued task of formation comes, once again, from the early church. The first task of postbaptismal training in the early church was to teach the mystery of the Eucharist. *The Apostolic Tradition* states that after the experience of communion, "the bishop shall explain the reason of all these things to those who partake."[1] This does not mean that communion is explained *as* they partake but in a period of time *after* they have experienced the Eucharist.

We also know that the newly baptized Christians were taught various matters pertaining to Christian vocation. *The Apostolic Tradition* states, "And when these things are completed [meaning baptism, communion, and entrance into the full life of the church] let each one hasten to do good works, and to please God and to live aright, devoting himself to the church, practicing the things he has learned, advancing in the service of the Lord."[2] I take these words to refer in a broad way to Christian vocation.

Taking our cue from *The Apostolic Tradition*, this chapter first explores how today's church may use this fourth period of faith formation to provide an introductory training in Christian vocation, particularly as it pertains to caring for the poor and needy, discerning personal gifts for use in the life of the local church, and understanding the Christian nature of work. Second, this chapter also explores how today's church may follow the early church practice of presenting the mystery of communion.

What Is Christian Vocation?

In today's postmodern world we must strive to be the church. I use the word *strive* intentionally in recognition of the countercultural calling of the church and the current pull of the culture to form the Christian community in its image. In this context we must ask, "How can the church and its people recover their Christian calling and vocation?" We begin by recovering the calling of the church. What is the church called to be in this postmodern culture and indeed in every culture? A. J. Conyers reminds us that "it is the modern individualistic word 'choice' that pulls us apart and 'vocation' that pulls us together."[3] We are to recall the church corporate as a called community and the baptized as a called people.

The Church as a Called Community

The corporate universal church and each local community must see itself as the "called out ones." God called Israel to be a witness to himself in the world. So also, God called the church into existence to be a special witness to him and his redeeming work. "You are a chosen people," Peter tells the Christians of the early dispersion, "a royal priesthood, a holy nation, a people belonging to God, that you may declare the praises of him who called you out of darkness into his wonderful light" (1 Peter 2:9). Here Peter states the *fact* of the church's calling. In the following verses he states the *substance* of this corporate calling: "Dear friends, I urge you, as aliens and strangers in the world, to abstain from sinful desires, which war against your soul. Live such good lives among the pagans that, though they accuse you of doing wrong, they may see your good deeds and glorify God on the day he visits us" (1 Peter 2:11–12). The church lives by an eschatological calling. Later when Peter writes about the coming of the Lord at the end of history, he asks, "Since everything will be destroyed in this way, what kind of people ought you to be? You ought to live holy and godly lives. . . . Make every effort to be found spotless, blameless and at peace with him" (2 Peter 3:11, 14). The church corporate does not simply *choose* to be countercultural, it is *called* to be countercultural, for, as Paul reminds us, "His intent was that now, through the church, the manifold wisdom of God should be made known to the rulers and authorities in the heavenly realms" (Eph.

3:10). (See chapter 9 for an interpretation of the church.) The members of every local church need to address the calling of the corporate church to be countercultural in its setting, whether in North America, Asia, Africa, Europe, or Latin American countries. As this question is discussed corporately, the issue will arise, "What is *my* calling in this church and to the world?"

Every Christian as Called

While the concept of Christian calling pertains to Israel and to the church as having a specific calling in this world, the concept of calling also applies to individuals. The concept of an individual calling is evident throughout all of Scripture—Abraham, Moses, David, the prophets, John the Baptist, and Paul all received distinct callings from God. Even Jesus, the Savior of the world, received an outward calling at his baptism, reiterated again in his Gethsemane prayer. We have a calling as well. It is to live in the pattern of the death and resurrection of Jesus Christ. Christians are called to discipleship, to Christian formation, to a life in the church, to a life in the world characterized by acts of mercy, and to a Christian understanding of their work.

We do not *choose* the Christian life; we are *called* to it. A. J. Conyers points out that "the idea of being called is a rather remarkable thing to say about persons and communities."[4] Our modern world has disparaged the idea of calling. It was Immanuel Kant who asked, "What is Enlightenment?" and answered it by saying, "It is the capacity to use one's intelligence without being guided by another." "Have courage to use your own intelligence! is therefore the motto of the Enlightenment."[5] *Choice* is the opposite of *calling*, and it has been, according to Conyers, the source "of the disorders that we associate with modern life—the social alienation, the breakdown of so-called mediating institutions such as the family and the violence that so marked the last century." All this is "tied to the loss of a sentiment of 'vocation.'"[6]

So what does it mean to have a Christian calling, a Christian vocation? It means, first, to be directed by God. A Christian calling comes outside of oneself. Conversion itself is a calling. We do not decide to transform ourselves. We hear the call to be open to God, to respond to his calling, and to submit and be obedient to him. We affirm God's calling in the acts of faith and baptism. We are called as disciples to follow Jesus, to be his witness. We are called to be his church, to be a member of his body, a servant to the community. The calling of God is to be a servant to the world, to be a witness to God's mission in the world, to speak of God's mighty acts of salvation, and to serve the poor and needy. This calling is also to serve God in our vocation, for work itself is a calling to the praise of God. This concept of calling and its ramifications in the church, in the world, and in work must be seen as a necessary part of initial Christian formation. We look briefly at each of these final areas of initial training by the church.

Our Calling in the Church

I recently watched *The Sopranos,* the popular HBO television program about the mob. The most interesting part of the program was the ceremony that initiated a new member into the mob family. It included a number of rituals that repudiated allegiance to any other mob as well as rituals of blood that affirmed a complete allegiance of life to the mob. Words were spoken to the effect that "the mob is your primary family. The mob is more important than your mother, your father, your wife, your children—you belong 100 percent to the mob. You will do what you are told; you will serve the mob gladly; you are owned by the mob . . . this is forever! Turn against the mob, squeal on the mob, disobey your orders . . . do any of these things and you will die. Now, if you can say yes to all this and mean it, repeat after me. . . ."

Immediately my mind went back to the Scriptures, to conversion, discipleship, Christian formation, and the rituals that express the transformation that takes place when a person comes into the full life of the church. I thought about the commitment early Christians were making—a commitment that led many of them to death. Then I thought of our current cultural concept of the church—how easy it is to come and go, to choose to participate or not. However, membership in the church is not a choice. It is a calling—a calling to participate; a calling to discover one's gift and offer it to the body of believers so that all may benefit.

This task of helping new Christians understand how the body of Christ works and where a gift fits into the whole is the task of equipping. Equipping is one of the goals of this period of Christian formation—knowing that the irreversible calling of the Christian is to be a full, conscious, committed, and active member of a local congregation. We are to help new Christians find and use their gifts, to find their place in the family. Paul Stevens, author of *Liberating the Laity*, reminds us that the word for equipping (Eph. 4:12) has a very interesting medical history—to equip is to put a bone or a part of the human body into right relationship with the other parts of the body so that every part fits thoroughly. It means to realign a dislocated limb.[7] Paul reminds us that even though there are different gifts, the Spirit gives these gifts "for the common good"

(1 Cor. 12:7). "The body," he reminds us, "is a unit, though it is made up of many parts" (1 Cor. 12:12).

Unfortunately, many church leaders are so controlling that they fear the unleashing of gifts. The top-down mentality sets up a clericalism in the church and frequently results in a consumer-driven community. The clergy become the dispensers of the goods, and the people become the consumers. No wonder people shop for a church. Clergy control has reversed the mandate of Paul. So the laity look for a church that gives them the best menu of goods. Some churches even blatantly use the term *menu* to seek to intentionally meet the needs of the spiritual buyer.

There are a number of church leaders who are seeking to reverse the consumer mentality and are returning to a body concept set forth by Paul. These churches are not *menu oriented* but *people oriented*. They see all God's people as ministers and find ways to help people find their gift and put it to use in the church. Some communities use a spiritual inventory approach in which new members are invited to consider their gift in light of all the gifts and are then given a place to serve.

I recently visited a start-up church that follows this method. I was most impressed with the middle-aged man who during the prayer time asked the congregation to pray for a friend of his son's whom they had taken into their home because his parents had evicted him. Then during the small group time I was particularly moved by his comments on the Scripture we were examining. Later that day I was talking to a person I had known for years and inquired about this man with obvious gifts of leadership and insight. "Oh him!" my friend said. "He became a Christian a year ago and has just blossomed among us. Our pastor, who has no issues about control, has helped him find his gifts and given him the support and space he has needed to do his calling. In addition to what you see, he has organized a Saturday morning Bible study for men that has been tremendously successful." Not every new Christian will have the gifts of teaching and leadership exhibited by this man, but every new Christian has a gift that needs to be released in ministry to the entire body. As Greg Ogden states, "Equipping pastors are committed to giving the ministry away."[8] During this fourth period of initial Christian formation, an aspect of ministry needs to be given to the new Christian as his or her calling to serve the body is discerned.

Called to Be a Servant to the World

Not only do all Christians have a calling in the church to serve the body, all Christians also have a calling to serve the world. This calling is almost always defined as a calling to serve the poor and needy. James is quite clear on this matter: "What good is it, my brothers, if a man claims to have faith but has no deeds? Can such faith save him? Suppose a brother or sister is without clothes and daily food. If one of you says to him, 'Go, I wish you well; keep warm and well fed,' but does nothing about his physical needs, what good is it? In the same way, faith by itself, if it is not accompanied by action, is dead" (James 2:14–17).

The same emphasis on a concern for the poor and needy was continued in the baptismal literature of the early church. In the *Didache*, a document written sometime between 50 and 120 A.D., new Christians were taught:

> Those who persecute good people, who hate the truth, who love lies, who are ignorant of the reward for uprightness, who do not "abide by goodness" or justice and are on the alert not for goodness but for evil, gentleness and patience are remote from them. "They love vanity," "look for profit," have no pity for the poor, do not exert themselves for the oppressed, ignore their maker, "murder children," corrupt God's image, turn their backs on the needy, oppress the afflicted, defend the rich, unjustly condemn the poor, and are thoroughly wicked. My children, may you be saved from all this.[9]

The issue of poverty in the second century was no different from the same issue in the twenty-first century. The church today as then is to teach Christians that they have a special calling to the poor and needy. Augustine, for example, explicitly taught new Christians to care for the poor. He taught, "Failure to share one's surplus with the needy is like theft."[10] According to William Harmless, "His command lay at the heart of Augustine's view of social justice."[11] Augustine regarded the surplus of the rich as belonging to the poor and admonished his hearers that "the surplus goods of the rich are the necessities of the poor. When you possess surplus goods, you possess the goods of others."[12]

Today's young leadership has a special concern for the poor and needy. Christian leaders who are "twenty something" (as well as others) are leading the church away from its fascination with the megachurch and returning to the city to build communities of faith among the poor and needy. For example, John and Debbie Wright felt called to begin a church in the city of Nottingham in 1996. When it was announced that they were going to start a new church, a number of people showed a great deal of interest in working with them. Eventually six couples "gave up their jobs, sold their homes, and moved to the city."[13] It was a year before they began a public Sunday meeting. Previous to the Sunday start they concentrated on servant evangelism, especially to the poor. Even though they had never done this before, they organized themselves to simply serve the needs of the neighborhood without any expectation of an immediate return. Other Christians joined them. Within three months forty-five people were organized into four house groups. They decided that each group would take $125 and use it to "bless the community." "On Mother's Day groups made bunches of flowers and went knocking on the doors of the single mothers they knew. They offered to do gardening or yard work or clean a person's house. They cleaned stairwells in rundown buildings and visited homes for the elderly, taking children along with them. They hosted street barbeques and neighborhood teas. From these contacts they began Alpha groups (a form of evangelism). Interest and attendance was high simply because this church had ministered to their needs."[14]

Each of these four groups continued to do something every two months. In that way some kind of servanthood was continually happening in the neighborhood. "Eventually a whole cross-section of the church began to minister to the poor, taking hats and gloves to people living on the street, presents to people in the hospitals, decorating a drop-in center . . . ministering to the poor."[15]

Eighteen months after the first Sunday service (which drew nearly one hundred people) a part-time assistant was brought on to lead the ministry to the poor. So many doors of ministry opened up that ministry to the poor simply exploded. The Wrights commented, "We felt God was speaking to us from Galatians, where Paul said 'all I ask is that you remember the poor.' We just thought 'Lord, if we invest here, we'll trust you with building the church,' and that's what happened."[16]

Soon a ministry was established in the local pub. People of the church bought drinks for strangers and sat with them and talked. Questions such as "Why are you doing this?" emerged and provided opportunities to present God's extravagant grace.

A ministry began in prison and also to street prostitutes. Debbie began to spend Friday mornings at an outreach place for prostitutes, talking to them about health issues, helping them with their problems, and introducing them to the Lord. Some of them came to the church. As one said, "They want to be part of a church where we're not just all about 'church' stuff, but we're out there doing what we can."[17]

Perhaps the key to ministry to the poor is to be "out there doing what we can." In every neighborhood there are needs. Each community should attempt to discover what those needs are and establish a ministry among the poor and needy simply because the church and Christians are called "to devote themselves to doing what is good" (Titus 3:8).

Work as a Calling

Another area in which new Christians need to recognize their calling is in their vocation. Unfortunately, many Christians function out of the secular/sacred dichotomy. They think of their work in the world as secular and their work for the kingdom as sacred. In this initial period of Christian formation we need to expose the fallacy of the secular versus sacred mentality. It is not only wrong headed, it is clearly biblically and theologically mistaken.

First, the doctrine of creation affirms the goodness of all that God has made. Even though the fall has occurred and the condition of sin has entered into all of life, work falls under the mandate of God. The Reformed community rightly points us back to what is called the "cultural mandate." Before the fall God spoke to Adam and Eve saying, "Be fruitful and increase in number; fill the earth and subdue it. Rule over the fish of the sea and the birds of the air and over every living creature that moves on the ground" (Gen. 1:28). The text tells us that "the LORD God took the man and put him in the Garden of Eden to work it and take care of it" (Gen. 2:15). After the fall the task of caring for the world and doing work became more complicated. "Cursed is the ground because of you; through painful toil you will eat of it all the days of your life. It will produce thorns and thistles for you, and you will eat the plants of the field. By the sweat of your brow will you eat your food until you return to the ground, since from it you were taken; for dust you are and to dust you will return" (Gen. 3:17–19). Though it may be difficult and full of challenges, the task of work is still a creational calling, even after the fall. For God "banished him from the Garden of Eden to work the ground from which he had been taken" (Gen. 3:23).

Work must also be seen in light of eschatology. God's incarnation in Jesus Christ within the fallen world is precisely for the purpose of paying the penalty for sin and overcoming the powers of evil that ravage and spoil God's creation. Work is therefore done not only as a mandate arising out of creation but also as a calling in light of God's mission and purpose for the world. Work anticipates that eschatological day of the new heavens and the new earth. Work arises out of the perspective that this world has been rescued by the death and resurrection of Jesus, and that Jesus is Lord over all creation. At the end of history as we know it, the shalom of God will rest over the entire world, and our work will be restored to its original purpose and more as in the Garden of Eden. In this way the church teaches new Christians to see all of life as the arena for their service to God. All legitimate areas of work are a service to God, a calling to work with God's creation in a redemptive way.

Christian vocation is not for this or that person here and there. Christian vocation is a full-time calling of God. All Christians are called of God to be the servants of God to each other in the church, to serve the world especially by caring for the poor and needy, and to do their work as unto the Lord. For the Christian there is no distinction between the secular and the sacred—all is sacred.

Teaching the Meaning of the Eucharist

The final ritual in this entire process of Christian formation is the Eucharist, also known as the Lord's Supper, the breaking of the bread, and communion. In the ancient church new Christians did not receive the Eucharist until after their baptism. In the great paschal vigil celebrated on the Saturday night that led into the great celebration of the resurrection on Easter morning, the new converts who had been made disciples were baptized. Immediately after baptism they experienced their first time to gather with the faithful to celebrate the Eucharist. Prior to this time there had been no explanation of the Eucharist. After this experience and during the seven weeks of the Easter season, the Eucharist and its meaning were explained. The early church waited to explain the Eucharist until after baptism because they were committed to the principle that experience precedes understanding.

The Eucharist in the Early Church

The earliest example of the Eucharistic celebration is given by Hippolytus in *The Apostolic Tradition*. A few comments about this presentation may help us understand what the Eucharist meant to early Christians. It may also provide us with a pattern for the teaching about communion in our own churches today.

First, here is the text from Hippolytus. I have added in bold the divisions of the structure.

The Lord be with you
And all shall say:
And with your spirit

The *Sursum Corda*
Lift up your hearts
we have them with the Lord
Let us give thanks to the Lord
it is fitting and right

111

Preface Prayer
We render thanks to you O God, through
your beloved child Jesus Christ, whom in
the last times you sent to us as savior and
redeemer and angel of your will.

[The *Sanctus* or Holy, Holy, Holy]

Prayer of Thanksgiving
Who is your inseparable word, through whom you made all things, and
in whom you are well pleased. You sent him from heaven into the virgin's
womb; and conceived in the womb, he was made flesh and was manifested as your Son, being born of the Holy Spirit and the virgin. Fulfilling
your will and gaining for you a holy people, he stretched out his hands
when he should suffer, that he might release from suffering those who
have believed in you. And when he was betrayed to voluntary suffering
that he might destroy death, and break the bonds of the devil, and tread
down hell, and shine upon the righteous, and fix the limit, and manifest
the resurrection. . . .

Words of Institution
He took bread and gave thanks to you, saying, "Take eat, this is my
body which shall be broken for you." Likewise also the cup saying,
"This is my blood, which is shed for you: when you do this you make
my remembrance."

The Remembrance
Remembering therefore his death and resurrection, we offer to you the
bread and the cup, giving you thanks because you have held us worthy to
stand before you and minister to you.

Prayer for the Work of the Holy Spirit
And we ask that you send your Holy Spirit upon the offering of your Holy
church; that gathering them into one, you would grant to all who partake
of the Holy things (to partake) for the fullness of the Holy Spirit for the
confirmation of faith in truth . . .

Closing Doxology
. . . that we may praise and glorify you through your child Jesus Christ,
through whom be glory and honor to you, to the Father and the Son with
the Holy Spirit, in your Holy church, both now and to the ages of ages.
(Amen)[18]

A book could easily be written on this ancient prayer, but here it will
be sufficient to simply point to the significance of the prayer's structure and mention the major theological themes without any attempt to

develop them. In this way we may gain an insight into the instruction offered in the early church and what we may teach today.

The structure of the prayer is triune. The preface prayer and the "Holy, Holy, Holy" is directed toward the Father. This part of the prayer begins with "lift up your hearts," which is a call to enter the heavens with the angels, the archangels, and the whole company of heaven and join them in the eternal song of "Holy, Holy, Holy!" Although the Sanctus is not in the prayer of Hippolytus, we know that it was sung at this point in the prayer from other sources. Here the early church reflects the worship of Revelation 4 and 5.

The second part of the triune structure of the prayer is directed toward the work of the Son. This part of the prayer, known as the "thanksgiving," sweeps through the entire story of God's work in history. It begins with the place of Jesus in the Godhead and recounts his incarnation and death, especially his victory over the powers of evil. The prayer then continues its historical recitation of salvation history with the words of institution followed by a statement on what it is that the church is thankful for—namely the death and resurrection and the privilege given to the church to make thanks.

Finally, the prayer turns to the work of the Holy Spirit and calls upon the Holy Spirit to make the church one and to confirm the faith through the reception of bread and wine. Then the prayer closes with a doxology to the Father, the Son, and the Holy Spirit.

The Ancient Response to Eucharistic Teaching

There is a very interesting document from the early church that records the response of ancient Christians to the instruction given about the Eucharist during the Easter season. The document, *Egeria: Diary of a Pilgrimage*, is a firsthand account of Egeria's travels and observations on the church in Jerusalem. The document contains no date, but scholars generally date its writing in the late fourth century.

For our purposes Egeria's comment on what happens during Easter week is most interesting. She explains how after worship the newly baptized assemble to hear the bishop explain the mysteries (baptism and Eucharist). She writes, "While the bishop is discussing and explaining each point, so loud are the voices of praise that they can be heard outside the church. And he explains these mysteries in such a manner that there is no one who would not be drawn to them, when he heard them explained."[19]

Although Egeria does not provide the exact content of instruction on baptism and Eucharist, it is obvious that the explanation must have accented the gospel. Both baptism and the Eucharist present the gospel in words and enactment.

A brief glance at the teaching of the Eucharist from the pre-Nicene period provides insight into the early church's understanding. The Fathers taught that continual spiritual nourishment was provided to believers at this great feast. First, it is clear from the writings of Justin Martyr in the middle of the second century that this is no empty symbol. Christ is really present in the bread and wine. He feeds us in the remembrance of his salvation. He nourishes us by his presence, which is accomplished through prayer. Justin presents this action as a mystery and does not express a theory about how it happens. One cannot find in his writings references to transubstantiation, consubstantiation, or any of the later theories of *how* God is made present in the bread and wine. It is a simple statement—Jesus is here in a real presence nourishing us in the faith as we feed on bread and wine. "For not as common bread and common drink do we receive these; but in like manner as Jesus Christ our savior, having been made flesh by the word of God, was made flesh and blood for our salvation, so likewise have we been taught that the food which is blessed by the prayer of His word, and from which our blood and flesh by transformation are nourished, is the flesh and blood of that Jesus who was made flesh."[20]

Next, Tertullian, the great Latin father of the church writing at the end of the second century, commented on how the bread and wine nourished new life. Referring to Jesus' own statement that he is "the Bread of Life," Tertullian noted how the reception of bread and wine is an action of abiding in Christ and he in us. The nourishment of bread and wine is a constant spiritual abiding in Christ. "In fact, Christ is our bread, for Christ is life and bread is life ('I am the bread of life,' Christ says; and just before that: 'the bread is the living word that comes down from heaven') . . . thus in asking for daily bread, we are asking to abide in Christ and not be separated from his body."[21]

Eucharistic Teaching Today

This brief excursion into the teaching of the Eucharist in the early church suggests several things for Eucharistic formation in today's church. First, it speaks to the frequency of the Lord's Supper. In the early church communion was celebrated every Sunday. The Reformers themselves called for weekly communion, but in most Protestant churches the Eucharist is celebrated on the first Sunday of the month. Some churches, particularly the Reformed, celebrate communion once a quarter. Why is there a decrease of communion among Protestants?

Briefly, Protestants rightly recovered the preaching of the Word, which had fallen into disuse in the late medieval period. Protestants also refrained from frequent communion because of the abuse of it by Catholic practice, particularly in the fourteenth and fifteenth centuries. Furthermore, the impact of print pushed leaders of the sixteenth century away from visual symbol to a concentration on words. Protestantism became a verbal community. Today, however, we are rediscovering the power of symbolic communication and reassessing the teachings of Scripture on the meaning of the Eucharist. Consequently many churches are increasing the frequency of communion—some from quarterly to monthly, others from monthly to biweekly, and a few to weekly.

Second, the early church practice of the Eucharist says something about the way we do communion. In recent years I have noticed how the Lord's Supper has been simplified in many churches. There is seldom a call to go up into the heavens and join with the eternal praise of the heavenly host, and there is almost never a prayer of thanksgiving for God's work throughout history culminating in the work of Christ. (Evangelicals will generally offer prayers of thanksgiving before taking the bread and the wine, but it is abbreviated.) Then there is seldom a prayer for the work of the Spirit in building the community and confirming faith. In brief, the trinitarian structure of table worship is neglected and, as a result, the remembrance of the full content of Father, Son, and Holy Spirit in salvation is not adequately presented. Consequently the Christian memory of the past and the Christian anticipation of the future is not fully rehearsed, and the nourishment of the soul through a recollection of God's saving acts does not take place as it should. Pastors and church leaders who want to provide spiritual nourishment at table worship need to recover both the basic structure and content of ancient table worship. There is no need to slavishly reproduce the exact wording of the ancient liturgy. Leaders should feel free to translate the content of these prayers into a form and language that communicates in the setting where they minister.

Finally, the early church practice of worship at the table says something about teaching on the Eucharist. Many people in our churches know very little about the meaning of the Eucharist because there is so little teaching on it from our pulpit or in small groups. Unfortunately, the church tends to follow the narcissistic bent of culture and concentrate on self-interest or self-improvement courses. "What can I get out of it?" dominates the choices we make. This market-driven and consumer mentality that runs so much of church life misses the sheer inner joy Christians feel and express when they learn the message of redemption and reconciliation that is spoken and enacted at the table. By neglecting to teach the great theme of redemption expressed at table worship we deny our new Christians the power of the table message that will provide them with a continual nourishment on the gospel and the presence of Jesus, the Bread of Life, who abides in them and they in him.

Conclusion

Let's go back to where we started—Christian vocation. This element of Christian formation ought not to be neglected. Many Christians feel Christianity is a private faith—it is me and God. This view is not biblical; it is often closer, if anything, to New Age spirituality. Yes, there is a private dimension to Christianity. It is personal; it does have to do with me and my relationship with God. Yet the Christian faith is also public and communal. Therefore new Christians need to be trained in the meaning of calling and vocation.

Christians are called to faith, called to the Christian community, called to be servants to the world, called to care for the poor and needy, and called to see their work as part of the cultural mandate, a participation in God's overall purpose for the world. What continually nourishes us in our calling is word and sacrament through which God verbally and symbolically feeds us with Jesus Christ, the Bread of the World. He abides in us through Word and table and we in him as we open ourselves to his teaching and presence.

New Christians are to be taught these truths so they know how to remain in him continually. A special resource for this stage of Christian formation is *Find Your Gift!*[22] It includes a biblical study on continuing in the faith, studies on finding and releasing your gifts in the church and to the world, and a study of the nourishment found in communion.

There is no rite of passage for this stage. The appropriate ritual, already discussed, in both its classical structure and content has been presented in this chapter. A visual presentation and training on how to celebrate communion in this ancient manner is included in the video *Ancient-Future Worship.*[23]

Table 14: What Is Christian Vocation?

Theme	Comments
The church as *called community*	The church is not a self-directed people. It lives under its calling by God to be a witness to God's involvement in history. Its calling is to be a countercultural, eschatological community of people.

Theme	Comments
Every Christian is *called*	Individual Christians are *called* to live in the pattern of the death and resurrection of Jesus. Discipleship is not a choice, it is a *calling,* and a divine one at that.
Our calling in the church	Each disciple is called to find and use his or her gift in the church for the good of the body.
Called to be a servant to the world	All disciples are *called* to care for the poor and needy.
Work as calling	All work is a calling under God. Disciples are called to serve God in every area of life—the home, the workplace, the neighborhood. All legitimate work and activity is ultimately in the service of God as it ministers to people and to the structures of our existence in the world.

Table 15: Teaching the Meaning of the Eucharist

Theme	Comments
Eucharist in the early church	The Eucharist is in praise of the triune God. Both content and structure are triune.
Ancient response to Eucharistic teaching	Christians are fed and nourished by the enactment of God's salvation at table worship.
Eucharistic teaching today	There is a need to recover the power of the enactment of the gospel at the Eucharist. It nourishes and feeds our relation to God, our vision of the world, and our place in it as disciples.

Questions for Discussion

1. Do the people of your church understand the calling of this church in this culture?
2. Do the people of your church understand their personal calling to live by the pattern of the death and resurrection of Jesus?
3. Has each person in your church found and put to work his or her own gift of ministry to this body?
4. How do the people of your church express their calling to be servants of the world?
5. Do the people of your church understand that their work and vocation is a calling from God?
6. Compare the content and structure of the ancient Eucharist to the structure and content of table worship in your church.
7. Do the members of your church experience table worship as an enactment of God's salvation and as a nourishment to their

everyday experience of living in the pattern of the death and resurrection of Jesus?

8. How committed is your church to doing ancient-future evangelism?

9. Have you considered how *Find Your Gift!* may be a helpful resource in teaching Christian vocation?

TWO

CULTURAL AND THEOLOGICAL REFLECTION

In part 2 of *Ancient-Future Evangelism* I address the underlying convictions of the process of Christian formation that I presented in part 1. My goal in part 2 is to identify the convictions that underlie ancient-future evangelism, to provide more information about its relevance for ministry in this world, and to invite the reader to a more sustained reflection on this ancient practice of Christian formation.

In Chapter 7 I address the first underlying conviction, which is to think more deeply about the world we evangelize. Since the late nineties a plethora of books, articles, conferences, and the like have warned us of the arrival of a new culture and have called us to reflect on the Christian message and how we communicate in the new world. My particular emphasis is on how our new culture bears a striking similarity to the culture of the first three centuries, showing, therefore, the value of drawing on the method of Christian formation in the early church.

My second underlying conviction is that we need to think more deeply about the Good News we preach, the message we deliver to those who are being discipled in the care of the church. I deal with this matter in chapter 8, again drawing on the early church. How did they interpret the Good News? What did they preach? The content I present from ancient Christianity is important because it proclaims the story of God's saving work in terms of creation, incarnation, and recreation. These themes connect with the current concerns articulated within missional Christianity. Missional Christianity understands the message not only as it pertains to individual salvation but also to the work of Christ extended to the entire creation. God has done in Jesus Christ what needs to be done to rescue individuals. Also, as Paul points out in Romans 8:18–22, God has delivered the creation from its bondage to decay. We all wait—creature and creation—with eager anticipation for God's completed work in the new heavens and the new earth. Biblical eschatology, as in the early church, points to the sovereignty of God over the events of history and to God's complete victory over the powers of evil. This emphasis not only recovers an essential theme of biblical Christianity, it also relates to the wars and rumors of war that dominate our present moment in history.

The third underlying concern of ancient-future evangelism is to focus on the church that tells the story. Chapter 9 draws both on ancient reflection and on the new materials presented by the current missional emphasis in the church. My focus is on the conviction that we no longer live in the world of Constantine. I urge that the purpose of the church is not to serve the politics of the world but the politics of Jesus—to witness in word and deed that the powers of evil have been overthrown and now stand under the judgment of God.

The fourth conviction, also articulated in chapter 9, is to show that the worship of the church proclaims and enacts the *Missio Dei* (mission of God). Worship signifies God's saving mission. Because worship focuses on God and what God has done in Jesus Christ to rescue the world, worship evangelizes, disciples, spiritually forms, and compels us to Christian vocation.

What I have attempted to do in these concluding chapters is theological reflection on Christian ministry within this culture. How do we engage with our changing culture? What is the message we proclaim? What is the effect of a church that embodies this message? How does the worship of this kind of church form new Christians and revitalize believers?

These are the issues the church currently faces. In these chapters and throughout the book I have asked these questions, and I have suggested that the ancient biblical and early church models point the way into the future. The following chapters simply ask you to think more deeply on the wisdom of the ancients for ministry in today's world.

Note in particular that the reflection I have asked for is a reflection that occurs in community, that this reflection is based on the historic language of the church, and that entrance into the community of the church and an embrace of the church's language constitutes a countercultural paradigm.

Ancient-future evangelism rejects the notion that the church and its faith must be defined by the language of the culture. True Christian formation occurs in a faith community whose language must be learned and lived.

7

THE WORLD WE EVANGELIZE

My father was born in 1900 and died in 1985. He grew up on a farm where he experienced the agricultural society, studied in Chicago where he experienced the industrial society, and died in a technological world.

In one lifetime my father experienced the three major cultures of history. That was dramatic! Since his death in 1985, however, there has been more change in the world than in all the previous centuries put together, and many people reading these words have gone through this time of swirling change. We have passed through the digital society into the internet society and stand on the edge of new and astounding breakthroughs in the near future. The point of this chapter is to look at our changing world and ask two questions: First, "What are the changes taking place in today's world?" and second, "How should we prepare to meet these changes to make disciples who remain steadfast in the faith?"

Our Post-Christian World

Much has been written about the advent of the new world in which we live. The themes have become familiar to most pastors and church leaders. For example, there is widespread knowledge of Jean-François Lyotard's definition of postmodernity as "incredulity toward meta-narratives."[1] *Meta* means "with" and *narrative* of course refers to story. According to Lyotard, it is very difficult to believe that there is one story, any story about the world and the human condition that can be true. This failure to have an overarching universal explanation of the world has led many to the hopeless conclusion that there is no meaning in this world other than the futile meaning each person can give to his or her life. All explanations of the world—scientific, religious, social—are of equal value and therefore of no value. Human existence cannot be explained and cannot be understood, and there is no one worldview that provides an ultimate explanation to this world and the life it sustains.

All of us have experienced this breakdown of the meaning of life. Many of us have relationships with people who live by stories different from our own or who live out of no story. Because of this change, it is now politically incorrect to challenge another person's story. Instead, based on the plethora of stories, a kind of eclecticism has occurred in society in which it is perfectly appropriate for each person to create his or her own story and defend it on the basis of feeling good about it. This is relativism.

In a recent *Nightline* town meeting with gay and lesbian teenagers, Ted Koppel asked, "What do you say when someone says to you, 'The Bible teaches that homosexuality is wrong'?" One teenager answered, "I really don't care. Everything is relative; no one has a right to judge me." Koppel responded by saying, "But the Bible does declare homosexuality to be wrong." The teenager responded, "It's right for me, so who are you or anyone else to judge me?" Koppel shot back, "Now you're judging me. Who gives you the right to do that?" The conversation ended right there.[2] In today's world when everything is relative, the only truth that anyone has is the truth he has for himself. There is no universal truth. Consequently, one may say, "The teenager is right. Koppel is right." What's right does not derive from any universal objective standard. What's right is only what's right for me.

In this way, truth has been reduced to privatism. Privatism teaches: "I have my truth; you have your truth; let's not bother each other with conflicting views. Please don't bother me with your truth even if you think you have reason to believe it."

Systems of truth that people once believed are now regarded as little more than social constructs created by people to control others. The prevailing opinion is that these constructs need to be deconstructed, abolished, and put behind us. The popular view is this: "The only thing that matters in the world is *me*. I am at the center of my own universe, and I determine my own existence, my own future."

While this mood of self-focused attention is dominant within our world, there are other cultural factors that make this a "post-everything" world. These factors include:

124

increased technology, especially the internet system;

the complexity of knowledge brought about by the information age and the accessibility of knowledge through computer retrieval systems;

the globalization of the world and the communication systems that provide us with instant knowledge of people and events;

the war on terrorism and the accompanying vulnerability and fear of the future;

the deterioration of our cities and the hopelessness resulting from the lack of meaningful work;

the prevalence of drugs and the power it has on the young;

the breakdown of the family and the moral permissiveness that is everywhere.

These issues and others have affected every geographical area and every people group whether rich or poor, whether Caucasian, African-American, Asian, Hispanic, Indian, or Slavic. In today's world, while some may be more isolated than others, none escape the influences of the new culture and world.

We Minister to This World

So to whom do we minister? We have no choice. We do not create our own world. We must minister to *this* world. But how? Some will choose to minister to this world by looking like the world. Others will seek to minister to this world by becoming a counterculture—a presence in this world that runs counter to the lifestyle of the prevailing worldview. As a countercultural community, Christians will proclaim that Christianity isn't primarily about me, my needs, my happiness, my fulfillment, my meaning. Countercultural Christianity is also not one of many stories or perspectives on life from which one can borrow this or that insight to create his or her own religion. Christianity makes a claim to truth, to universality. It challenges all prevailing wisdoms and calls people into radical faith and discipleship. It holds a particular understanding of the human condition, a specific view of salvation, and a certain hope for the history of the world. To minister to *this* world Christians need to assert the countercultural nature of Christianity and seek points of contact with people who live in this post-Christian culture. The fact that this world is post-Christian and postmodern may have changed our culture and altered the rules for knowledge, but it hasn't changed the human heart. Saint Augustine's statement remains true: "Thou hast made us for thyself, O God, and our souls are restless until they find their rest in thee."[3]

Consequently the church must find new ways to tap into this restlessness. It needs to break through the veneer of our post-Christian and postmodern culture to connect with the restless heart that longs for truth, for mystery, for community, and for a relationship with God that provides wisdom and direction for life. But where do we go to find out how to make these connections? Where do we go for a model of Christian faith and discipleship pertinent for this world? I have proposed to find an answer to that question in the biblical and ancient era of the Christian faith.

Similarities with the World of the First Three Centuries

Have we forgotten that Christianity was birthed in a pagan world that was hostile to the faith? It was first of all a world of religious pluralism. Larry Hurtado puts the rise of Christianity in a setting where religion was "varied, prominent, pervasive and popular." We misunderstand the Roman world of early Christianity if we do not recognize how thoroughly religious it was. "It is difficult," writes Hurtado, "to point to any aspect of life in that period that was not explicitly connected with religion."[4] He goes on to show how the cycle of life from birth to death was marked by religious ceremony. Furthermore, every aspect of private and public life was saturated with religious ceremony. A unique feature of this religious culture was that everybody's deity was acknowledged. No deity was challenged. *Religious relativism was sacred.*

Christianity came into this setting with an exclusive message. It viewed all the religions of the Roman Empire as suspect, especially the assumption that Caesar is Lord. Christians proclaimed "Jesus is Lord" and no other is to be worshiped or served. Tertullian admonished, "It is not asked who is ready to follow the broad way, but who the narrow."[5] To proclaim that Jesus alone was to be worshiped was a countercultural act that resulted in persecution.

Christians were seen as political anarchists, a social menace, a scourge on society. Yet, pagans came to Christ in droves, and many knew that their conversion to Christ and his church meant persecution and possible death. Yet they came. Why? What was it about the Christianity of the early church that engendered such discipleship and Christian commitment?

We live in a similar world—a world that is secular and pagan yet thoroughly religious, even superstitious. *Christianity Today* recently did a feature article on the popularity of Oprah and her religious eclecticism.

According to author LaTonya Taylor, "Oprah's show has normalized a generic spirituality that perceives all religions as equally valid paths to God."[6]

The widespread presence of numerous religions in our society has only begun. A recent *Atlantic Monthly* issue featured an article entitled, *Oh, Gods!* in which author Toby Lester presented the thesis that "an explosion of new religions will shake the 21st century." Today's world, he claims, "is awash in religious novelty, flux, and dynamism as it has ever been—and religious change is, if anything, likely to intensify in the coming decades."[7]

What of Christianity? How will it fare in a world of pluralism, a world of many paths to God? Will its exclusivity engender a new wave of persecution? According to a recent *World* magazine report, persecution of Christians around the world is on the increase. Author Marvin Olasky reports, "Many journalists have displayed anti-Christian bigotry, the one type of bigotry still allowed and even esteemed among many academic and media leaders." He shows that a newspaper as highly respected as the *New York Times* "would have us believe that conservative Christians are major threats to domestic tranquility."[8]

We now live in a culture in which all beliefs are equally regarded except that one belief, Christianity. Christians today, as in the early church, will be persecuted and disregarded because they will not subscribe to the cult of religious relativity nor affirm religions that subscribe to the notion that all paths lead to God.

How does one evangelize and disciple new Christians in a culture in which Christianity is mocked for its exclusivity? The early Christians were not only able to survive, they brought paganism to its knees and conquered the empire for Christ. How did they do that? Can we adapt and translate their evangelism and discipleship for our postmodern world? If so, what kind of church will it take to do it?

The Church in the Post-Christian World

Broadly speaking, there are three views of the church in culture: (1) the church is identified with culture; (2) the church is against culture; (3) the church transforms culture. These three statements are a reflection of the tension the church has had with culture from its very beginning in the New Testament era.[9]

The church is identified with culture in the sense that its people live normal lives—they marry, have children, buy food and goods in the marketplace, live in houses, pay their taxes, and live through the cycles and patterns of life just like everybody else. We may refer to this as an identification with the structures of existence that order and organize our lives in the world.

Yet Christians are also against culture because they are called upon to live lives that are different. They are not to be shaped by lives of unrighteousness (Rom. 6:12) or by the ways of the old man (Col. 3:5–9), nor are they to walk according to the flesh (Gal. 5:19–21). Instead the Christian life is shaped by being servants of righteousness (Rom. 6), by living according to the new man (Col. 3:12–17), and walking after the Spirit (Gal. 5:22–26). In these passages, Christians are urged not to succumb to the powers but to wrestle with the powers of darkness (Eph. 6:12) and proclaim the victory of Christ over them. Consequently, Christians are aliens, strangers, and sojourners in this world. They live in opposition to the values of this world.

Third, because Christians live in the structures of the world, in a countercultural way they are a transforming presence. The church becomes a transforming presence in culture when Christians live by Christian values in the various structures that rule our lives—political, economic, institutional, educational, medical, etc. Christians make these structures function better by their presence within them and by the "salt and light" effect that they have upon them. Christians have a profound effect upon culture as they live in this paradoxical relationship—identified with it, yet living in antithesis to its ideologies.

The Present Cultural Shift

How then should we live in this post-Christian culture? The current cultural shift is in reality an extension of the sixties revolution in that it has taken the nihilism of that period to its logical conclusion and proclaimed there is no universal explanation of the world and of life. In today's world, all ideas, all concepts, all systems of power, all ideologies, all answers are suspect. The only thing you can count on is yourself—your ideas, your morality, your goals.

This kind of autonomy and relativism is very dangerous. A world torn by violence, chaos, and the loss of meaning is a perfect setting for the rise of a dictator who promises peace and stability in exchange for blind obedience and uniformity. Interestingly, it is also a social setting not too different from that of the first centuries into which Christianity emerged. In the ancient world, paganism produced no moral values and no meaning. The Roman government ruled with an iron hand as it was threatened by violence in the streets, by war, and by general instability.

In the early church, Christians took a strong anticultural stance. They were good citizens; they were peaceful, paid their taxes, and cared for widows and orphans. Yet they called people to enter into a community of people who *differed* in life and thought from the pagan ways. They offered them a new life in a new community, the church.

A similar kind of phenomenon is occurring today. Christians are beginning to respond to this culture with a countercultural Christianity, and a missional view of the church is emerging. The people who hold this view believe the society around them is their mission field. They want to work in their particular neighborhood, in their city, village, and county. Consequently, their approach to ministry is servanthood. They want to know, "How can I serve the spiritual, physical, educational, and psychological needs of this neighborhood?" For them worship tells and acts out the great story of God's involvement in the world to rescue the world from its fallen condition. People gather to interact with this story, to learn, to be formed spiritually by it, and to live in obedience to Jesus Christ as Lord. Evangelism is seen as a process, a journey that takes a person through stages of spiritual development into a deeper walk with God. Education is more than learning details of knowledge. It is character formation—learning to live in obedience to the way of Jesus. Youth work is not party after party, but prayer, Bible study, and worship. In this way the missional church is more countercultural than the traditional church of the fifties and the contemporary postsixties church.[10]

The emerging generation of missional leaders grew up inside the culture of the late twentieth century. They were caught between the rise of the postmodern "everything goes" culture and a Christianity that looked more and more like the culture of this matrix, but a new beginning for the evangelical church is emerging. The missional church rejects the association of Christianity with American values and the association of the church with entertainment, marketing, and corporate business models. The missional church is reading both Scripture and culture with new eyes. It sees that what is demanded by the Christian faith is more than being a good, upright citizen. It sees the church as something different from the smooth corporate model of business. This emerging church calls for an honest, authentic faith that seeks to be church in the way of a more radical discipleship.[11]

The missional leadership calls for a countercultural Christianity that challenges cultural norms and standards. It is calling for a Christianity that stands for a different way of life as it responds to the cultural changes of the twenty-first century.

Responding to the Post-Christian Culture

Emerging leaders think the current cultural changes may be as far-reaching as other shifts in Western society such as the fall of Rome and the rise of the medieval era or the birth of modernity out of the Renaissance and the Reformation. No one knows for sure, but there is agreement that this new era demands two simultaneous approaches. The first is to *stand over against* the world where the Christian faith is in conflict with cultural values. The second is to *make connections* with the culture where Christian faith and values are not challenged.

The Call to Stand Over Against Culture

The first issue to deal with is how and where the Christian faith radically differs from the present assumptions of culture. Three matters in particular stand out: philosophical, ethical, and spiritual relativism.[12]

Philosophical relativism is the teaching that there is no one story that explains the world. I have already mentioned how Jean-François Lyotard captured this teaching in his description of postmodernity as the "incredulity toward meta-narratives."[13] By this he means to say that in this complex and pluralistic world it is impossible to believe that any one story is true for everybody. This relativistic view of life has filtered down into every aspect of life. In religious conversations, it is not politically correct to say that there is one way, the way of Jesus. There is nothing that will raise the ire of someone more than this teaching. I remember, for example, years ago when the hundredth archbishop of Canterbury, Archbishop Ramsey, was in the United States and was interviewed on the *Johnny Carson Show*. The next person to be interviewed ignored Johnny Carson and instead turned to the archbishop and said, "Archbishop, there is one thing about your viewpoint I don't like. You say there is only one way to God. I don't believe that! I think there are many ways to God and to assert exclusivity is arrogant."

I wondered what the archbishop would say. "My dear," he said (this was in the days before feminism), "I have never said there is only one way. It was Jesus who said it. As a follower of Jesus, I have no right to contradict him. I am called to be faithful to him and to his teaching."

The archbishop gave a good answer and really the only appropriate biblical one. In the end, Christianity has an exclusive message. "I am the way, the truth and the life," said Jesus. As Christians we have no freedom to change his message into, "I am one of the ways." In postmodern philosophical thought, the assertion that Jesus is the way puts the faith into a countercultural position.

This is equally true of the Christian rejection of *ethical relativism*.[14] "Do your own thing so long as *you* feel good about it," or the postmodern shrug followed by, "Whatever," is not a Christian view of things. Sure, there are matters that do fall into these categories, but the Christian faith is clear about what needs to be "put off" and "put on." As Ted Koppel once said of the Ten Commandments, "They are not ten suggestions, you know."

There are many lifestyle matters that are central to Christianity. What Moses, Jesus, or Paul taught about the way of righteousness are not matters to be disputed and relativized but obeyed and lived.

The third type of relativism that Christians reject is the *spiritual relativism* of the day.[15] I have already referred to the "religion of Oprah" and to the pervasive influence of the New Age Movement. This religion is not the faith of the Bible, and there is no way that Christianity can affirm its theoretical assumptions. Christianity holds to a very different view of creation, redemption, and spirituality than that of the New Age. David Pendleton, a young evangelical minister in Kansas City who ministers to many younger people, told me he will not use the words *spiritual formation* because of its distortion by New Age proponents. To differentiate Christian spirituality from New Age spirituality, he uses the term *Christian formation*.

Christians cannot embrace philosophical, ethical, and spiritual relativism. Christians have a story about the world that goes from creation, to the fall, to the incarnation, and to the new heavens and the new earth. If this story is relativized, we tear at the heart of the Christian message. The same can be said about Christian ethics. Christians affirm an objective standard of right and wrong articulated in the Bible and upheld by the experience of God's people throughout history. In the face of ethical relativism Christianity is dramatically countercultural. The same is to be said about the prevailing New Age spirituality. It is not Christian in its foundational beliefs. Christian spirituality stands over against the popular spiritualities of the New Age Movement.

Making disciples in a post-Christian world is a countercultural activity: Christians are to hold to the conviction that Christianity is the one true faith, affirm ethical absolutes, and embrace a unique spirituality that is not to be confused with New Age God talk.

The Call to Make Connections with Culture

Second, there is another side to a Christian relationship with culture that has to do with current cultural revolutions. The missional church makes a distinction between those areas of cultural change that demand a countercultural response and those areas of change that primarily

131

alter the social context in which the church does ministry. Christians do not reject changes that do not affect the nature of the faith. Instead, the church *engages* with these shifts in culture.

To put it another way: How do the current revolutions that are bringing us into a new cultural situation provide connecting points for Christian communication? What cultural revolutions can Christians affirm and take into account in the communication of an unchanging message? There are at least seven changes in culture that Christians may affirm and with which they may engage.

The first is the death of the Christian era and the *rise of the post-Christian era*.[16] When Constantine became a Christian in 311 A.D., he put the church in a privileged place. The church gradually made alliances with the state, and the concept of a Christianized state was born. In the United States the state has generally supported the church, and the church in turn has served the state as its chaplain, enjoying a privileged place in society. However, that place of privilege is now decreasing due to the impact of secularization and the subsequent rise of numerous religions. The connecting point for the church is that it is now in a position in which it can be more clearly defined as countercultural. In order for the church to make a connection with post-Christendom, it must recognize the death of the so-called Christian era, affirm that the church now exists in a post-Christian world, and make a commitment to minister to this world.

The second revolution is the current *epistemological shift*.[17] The modern reliance on reason and science has been called into question by the changes taking place in science and philosophy. In the modern world, Christians followed the rational and scientific method of knowing truth and built systems of knowledge based on methodologies drawn from science and reason. Some evangelical Christians today regard the rational and scientific support of the faith sacrosanct, but the next generation leadership does not affirm this position. For the most part, the new generation of leaders prefer to present Christianity through narrative forms of theology and an embodied apologetic. These new (actually very old) ways of presenting the faith obviously affect the way evangelism and discipleship is done in this postrational and postscientific dependent culture.

The third significant revolution that has changed the way Christianity is presented is the *communication revolution*.[18] Communications have always impacted the way the church delivers its message. For the first thousand years the church's faith was expressed orally, especially through the liturgy. The advent of print shifted Christian communication to the verbal, more cognitive side. Protestant worship has been particularly cognitive. The birth of television has restored imagery, and the arts and the arrival of the internet have moved society to a more interactive approach to communication. The rise of the visual, symbolic, and interactive nature of communications affects the new approach to evangelism and discipleship.

Next is the *globalization* of our world, which has resulted in the diversity of people in our churches—the diversity of color and of age.[19] The church now has the opportunity to express its global nature. The body of Christ is from "every tribe and nation," and it represents every age group. A concerted effort on the part of the church to break with the old notion of a *targeted audience* and *generational ministries* will allow the church to be a community of people who represent the global nature of the body of Christ. Here again is another way to connect with this culture.

The *environmental revolution* also provides a point of contact for today's Christians.[20] The first article of the Apostles' Creed is, "I believe in God the Father Almighty, Creator of heaven and earth." In a recent discussion with Steve Hulsey, a postgraduate student at Fuller Seminary, he pointed out that we evangelicals typically begin our discussions with non-Christians by pointing out our fallen human condition. Steve rightly argued that Christianity begins with God, creation, and the fall. In the postmodern world there is a need to start with God's act of creation, with God's love of creation, and with God's intent to rescue the created order. In this way, Christians are able to connect with the new concern for the care of creation. (This point of contact in no way denies our fallen condition, as I will show later.)

The *war on terrorism* represents an opportunity for the church and its witness. In *The New Terrorism*, Walter Laqueur speaks of terrorism as "one of the gravest dangers facing mankind" and laments that while "science and technology have made enormous progress . . . human nature, alas, has not changed."[21] It is no longer uncommon to speak of evil and to point to the evil and hate that lurks in people's hearts. Terrorism has had the effect of pointing to the fallen human condition. While this message seems to focus on the terrorist in particular, its obvious application to the human condition of us all is apparent. Here, then, is another point of connection between the Christian faith and our current postmodern cultural condition.

The *technological revolution* has also affected the shape of culture and our everyday lives.[22] New technologies have reshaped global culture and the economy of the world. It has affected how local business is conducted, how relationships are established and maintained, and how the church engages with culture. The church must connect with this culture, showing both how technology may be used in a redeeming way and how technology may demonize and control our lives.[23]

The paradoxical situation of Christianity is clear: Christians reject the ideologies of culture (because Christianity is an antithesis to them), yet Christians must find ways to make connections with this culture (because we live in this culture, not another). In this way the tension between the rejection of the ideologies of culture and the embrace of living in this culture allows the Christian to be a transforming presence in this post-Christian culture.

Conclusion

I have suggested that the issue of evangelism and discipleship must be understood in the context of a post-Christian culture. I have argued that we live in a new world and that the church must minister in this world, not another. Because this world is like the era in which Christianity initially took root, a clue for how to minister in this world may be taken from the ancient world. Like the ancient world, this new world is characterized by philosophical, ethical, and spiritual relativism. Consequently, today's church must be countercultural by virtue of its universal story, absolute ethical standard, and Christ-centered spirituality.

However, there are points of contact that can be made with our post-Christian world. The new generation of leaders and many from other generations as well readily affirm that we live in a post-Christian era, that changes in epistemology and communications theory need to be taken into account in the way Christianity is presented. Revolutions like globalization, the environmental crisis, terrorism, and new technologies are to be acknowledged, understood, and engaged with as the gospel is communicated in a new context, very different from the culture of the twentieth century.

We evangelize in a new world. We bring an unchanging message to a changing culture. How we communicate this message in our post-Christian world is the question this book has addressed. I have suggested that we return to the ancient sevenfold process adapted for use in our evangelical churches. I am persuaded that our culture is ripe for this very old yet very new form of evangelism and Christian formation.

However, I also believe we must ask once again, "What is the gospel we preach to this world?" The answer to this question lies in the ancient and classical interpretation of the Christian faith. This interpretation is thoroughly biblical, was very effective in the pre-Christian world, and needs to be rediscovered for the post-Christian world of today.

Table 16: Our Post-Christian World

Theme	Comments
We live in a new world.	The dominant theme of the new world is *relativism*.
We minister to *this* world.	The church will most effectively minister to this world by being a counterculture, not by adapting the ways of culture.
The post-Christian world is very much like the world of the first three centuries.	This world is characterized by religious pluralism. Christianity, as in the Roman world, must maintain the exclusivity of its message.
Models of the church in culture	The church is *against* culture (its ideologies). The church *identifies* with culture. The church *transforms* culture.
The present cultural shift	Every church exists in a missional setting and is called to serve *its* cultural context.
How the emerging church is responding to the present post-Christian culture	The missional church stands *against* philosophical, ethical, and spiritual relativism. This is the countercultural expression of the church. The church is *engaged* with cultural changes such as the shift into the post-Christian era, the epistemological shift to experience, the communication shift to the internet, the impact of globalization, the environmental revolution, the war on terrorism, and the rise of technology.

Questions for Discussion

1. How has your congregation been affected by relativism?
2. How does your congregation reflect the countercultural nature of the church?
3. Discuss the three models of church and culture: against; identified with; transforms. Which model best describes the emphasis of your community?
4. Does your congregation have a *missional* self-understanding?
5. How does your congregation deal with:
   - philosophical relativism (pluralism of faith)
   - ethical relativism (no objective standards of right and wrong)
   - spiritual relativism (New Age view of spirituality)
6. How does your congregation engage with the changing culture in these areas:
   - post-Christian culture
   - shift to subjectivity
   - participatory communication

- globalization
- terrorism
- technology

7. In order to make disciples in a post-Christian era, what are the issues your church will need to face?

8

THE STORY WE TELL

I was taught from the cradle that John 3:16 was the nutshell of the Bible, the most important truth of Christianity, the creed from which my faith should never depart. I believed it then; I believe it now. As I grew older and more mature in the faith, and especially as I began to read the early church fathers, I saw that John 3:16 was the *Missio Dei* (mission of God) and was an invitation to embrace a sweeping story that encompassed the whole of history.

There is one word that captures the heart of this story—the word *recapitulate*. The word appears in Paul's letter to the Ephesians. Here Paul identifies Christ as the one who will "bring all things [recapitulate] in heaven and on earth together under one head" (Eph. 1:10). This grand vision is the substance of John 3:16. God in Christ is the one who recapitulates, that is, restores and renews the entire universe. Recapitulation is expressed by Paul in the great hymn sung by the Colossian community: "Through him to reconcile to himself all things" (Col. 1:20). In another hymn sung at the Philippian church, God's people proclaim that "every tongue [will] confess that Jesus Christ is Lord, to the glory of God the Father" (Phil. 2:11). This biblical message of the recapitulation of all things is the Good News fleshed out by the early church fathers. In the theology developed by the fathers of the church, they interpret the full meaning of the word *recapitulate* and tell the whole story of God's mission from creation to incarnation to re-creation.

The underlying theme of recapitulation and indeed of the entire Bible is that the whole creation is under sin and death. Yet God's mission is to free creation (nature and people) from death and deliver creatures and creation into life—life in this world and life eternal. This message is the theme of the great hymn in the opening of Paul's letter to the church at Colosse: "For he has rescued us from the dominion of darkness and brought us into the kingdom of the Son he loves, in whom we have redemption, the forgiveness of sin" (Col. 1:13–14).

Sin results in death. "Just as sin entered the world through one man, and death through sin . . . in this way death came to all men, because all sinned" (Rom. 5:12). Death is all around us—in family and friends, in nature and culture, in social and business relationships. Death permeates the very structure of existence. Death is in the hopelessness, the weariness, the despair of troubled lives, and a world torn by war and strife. Nothing lasts; everything ends. There is no permanence to life. It is a catastrophe of eternal consequences! John writes that God's mission in the face of death is that we "should not perish."

The opposite of death is life. God's reply to death is life. The psalmist cries out in praise, "You renew the face of the earth" (Ps. 104:30). The prophet Ezekiel envisions dry bones coming to life (Ezek. 37:1–14). The apostle Peter, by the inspiration of the Spirit, proclaims on the day of Pentecost that new life has come in Jesus:

This man was handed over to you by
God's set purpose and foreknowledge;
and you, with the help of wicked men,
put him to death by nailing him to the
cross. But God raised him from the dead,
freeing him from the agony of death, because
it was impossible for death to keep its hold on him.
David said about him:

"I saw the Lord always before me.
Because he is at my right hand,
I will not be shaken.
Therefore my heart is glad and my tongue rejoices;
my body also will live in hope,
because you will not abandon me to the grave,
nor will you let your Holy One see decay.
You have made known to me the paths of life;
you will fill me with joy in your presence."

Acts 2:23–28

The Scriptures everywhere declare that God's mission, the *Missio Dei*, is to rescue humanity and indeed all creation from death. His purpose is to reign as Lord of creation.

Salvation to the ends of the earth is also the vision of the early church fathers. It is the vision for every time and the vision for our time. We live in a disintegrating world surrounded by death and decay. The message of God for this world is one of hope, renewal, and restoration. His *Missio Dei* arises out of the heart of the triune God. The story of the triune God rescuing the world from death and restoring life is the central story of the Bible and the story that gave rise to the classical Christian message and mission. The story is told through the acts of God in history—the acts of creation, incarnation, and re-creation. It cannot be told apart from sin, the origin of death, the struggle between all that is death and all that is life. God's mission takes our death into himself and destroys it so that he may give us his own life, calling us into eternal community with the Godhead. This is the message the church has to offer to this post-Christian world—a message of redemption and hope.

Throughout history there has been some question about where we should begin with the story of God's redeeming work. Should we begin by probing the thought of God in his eternal decrees? Should we begin with creation? Is it best to enter this story by getting in touch with the fallen human condition?

Incarnation, Death, and Resurrection

This chapter begins with the approach of Paul and the early church fathers. In this hermeneutic the entrance to the Christian story is through the work of Jesus Christ. It is only through Jesus Christ that the purposes of creation, the problem of the fall, and the hope of the new heavens and the new earth are known. Through him the purposes of God the Father and the work of the Spirit in the church and its worship become clear. We begin, then, with the story of Jesus revealed through the incarnation, death, and resurrection, for this is the story that evangelizes and makes disciples of Jesus. (What follows is the gospel story that needs to be taught to new Christians in their process of formation. It captures the teaching of the Apostles' Creed.)

Jesus' Mission according to the Biblical Writers

The mission of God through Jesus is announced with the incarnation. John interprets this event as the Word taking on human flesh and dwelling among the people of the world (John 1:14). When Jesus began his ministry, he proclaimed that the kingdom of God had arrived. Mark tells us that Jesus proclaimed throughout Galilee that "the time has come. . . .

The kingdom of God is near. Repent and believe the good news!" (Mark 1:15). The frequent references to the kingdom in the Synoptic Gospels and in John clearly point to the arrival of the kingdom as the central message of Jesus. Jesus has come to overthrow the powers of evil and to exercise his rule over all creation.[1] What must he do to accomplish this mission? The New Testament writers present a clear and unambiguous answer to this question.

First, Jesus must bind the powers of evil. Exegetes have pointed to the conversation of Jesus with the Pharisees recorded in Matthew 12: 22–37, in which the Pharisees accused Jesus of casting the demons out by the power of Beelzebub. Jesus' answer to them was clear. He has entered into the strong man's house (the world, Beelzebub's domain) and has tied him up (bound him, constricted his movement). Thus Jesus can say, "If I drive out demons by the Spirit of God, then the kingdom of God has come among you" (v. 28).

Second, God's mission to this world cannot be accomplished without a sacrifice for sin.[2] This truth was taught to Israel through the sacrificial system. The writer of Hebrews interpreted the Old Testament Hebrew system of sacrifice as a foreshadow of what was to come. Referring to the blood of bulls and goats in the former covenant, the author of Hebrews declares, "How much more, then, will the blood of Christ, who through the eternal Spirit offered himself unblemished to God, cleanse our conscience from acts that lead to death, so that we may serve the living God!" (Heb. 9:14).

Third, by his sacrificial death Jesus has overcome the powers of evil.[3] Paul clearly states this truth to the Colossian community: "He forgave us all our sins . . . he took it away, nailing it to the cross. And having disarmed the powers and authorities, he made a public spectacle of them, triumphing over them by the cross" (Col. 2:13–15).[4]

Furthermore, Jesus showed us how to live a life of servanthood. When he took the towel and washed the feet of his disciples, he taught that meaning in life does not come from power but from servanthood. This servant model was demonstrated supremely in his sacrifice on the cross. "This is how we know what love is: Jesus Christ laid down his life for us. And we ought to lay down our lives for our brothers" (1 John 3:16).[5]

The life, death, and resurrection of Jesus is captured in the image of the second Adam. Jesus reverses the sin of the first Adam. He bore the penalty of death arising from the sin of the first Adam. He conquered the powers of evil unleashed in the world due to Adam's rebellion. He took the failure of Adam's life to live as a servant to his neighbor and showed us how to live. He did all this, Paul reports, "so that, just as sin reigned in death, so also grace might reign through righteousness to bring eternal life through Jesus Christ our Lord" (Rom. 5:21).[6]

Through his sacrifice for our sin and his victory over the powers of evil, Jesus accomplished the recapitulation of all things. We now await the second coming when, as the great hymn of the Philippian church proclaims, "At the name of Jesus every knee should bow, in heaven and on earth and under the earth, and every tongue confess that Jesus Christ is Lord, to the glory of God the Father" (Phil. 2:10–11). The Colossian hymn declares that in Christ all things have been reconciled to God, "all things, whether things on earth or things in heaven" (Col. 1:20). Mission accomplished! Death has been vanquished. Life has been restored. The recapitulation of all things is done.

Jesus' Mission according to the Early Fathers

Now let us turn to the early church fathers to see how they remained faithful to the message of God's reconciling work in Jesus Christ. Irenaeus, the second-century apologist against the Gnostics, clearly expressed Jesus' mission to the world: "So the Lord now manifestly came to his own, and born by his own created order which he himself bears, he by his obedience on the tree renewed and reversed what was done by disobedience in connection with a tree. . . . He therefore completely renewed all things."[7]

Irenaeus summarizes four very clear biblical motifs. First, God became incarnate. The texts of the New Testament that the "Word became flesh and made his dwelling among us" (John 1:14) are captured by these words of Irenaeus: "The Lord now manifestly came to his own, and born by his own created order which he himself bears."

There is a tendency to think that God *stepped* into time, space, and history to rescue people from the world. The early church understood the incarnation in a deeper way. God did not merely *step into history*. God became flesh, became his creation, became time, space, and history. When he took on human flesh, God took on Adam to recapitulate Adam. God also took on the world to recapitulate the entire creation. (He participated in the very same life in the world in which we all participate. He was truly man, born of a woman, real flesh, connected with all creation, and passed through all the stages of life—infancy, adolescence, maturity, and death.) His incarnation then was an incarnation into humanity and thus being fully human was an incarnation into the very stuff of life in this world.

Second, God's incarnation into our reality was a demonstration of love for us in that "while we were still sinners, Christ died for us" (Rom. 5:8). Adam's disobedience through his exercise of freedom against God set into motion that chain of events that brought sin, death, and condemnation to Adam's posterity and to the whole creation. God's answer to evil took place on the tree. Here, by the sacrifice of Christ, an atonement was made for sin. Here at the cross and empty tomb Jesus is the Victor over sin and death. Here at the cross Jesus shows us through his suffering an example of how we are to live in a life-giving way through powerlessness. His work on the tree is the means by which Jesus reversed the sin of Adam at the tree. One tree represents disobedience, sin, and death. The other tree represents obedience, sacrifice for sin, and life.

Through God's mission in Jesus, God has saved both creatures and creation. By his incarnation into a humanity and a created order under the judgment of death he "renewed and reversed what was done by disobedience on the tree."[8] Here Irenaeus captures once again the Pauline doctrine of recapitulation. For "just as the result of one trespass was condemnation for all men, so also the result of one act of righteousness was justification that brings life for all men. For just as through the disobedience of the one man the many were made sinners, so also through the obedience of the one man the many will be made righteous" (Rom. 5:18–19). God through Christ has reversed the human situation and extended salvation to creation. Thus Paul states, "The Creation itself will be liberated from its bondage to decay and brought into the glorious freedom of the children of God" (Rom. 8:21).

For this reason the final result of the mission of God is that "He therefore completely renewed all things."[9] Here Irenaeus refers to the eschatological vision of a renewed creation, the vision of Isaiah and Revelation. The final result of God's mission through Jesus is that God has reclaimed the world and God's reign extends over all creation.[10] Because the work of Christ is cosmic—having to do with everything from creation to re-creation—we turn now to interpret creation, the problem of the fall, the presence of evil, and God's redemption.

Creation and the Fall

Both the biblical writers and the interpreters of biblical tradition point to the mission of God in Jesus Christ as the work of recapitulation. God so loved the world that he gave his only begotten Son to restore the world to himself. This mission and its result implies that something has gone wrong in God's creation. In order to fully understand the recapitulation we must look at creation and the fall.

We begin with two questions: Where did we come from, and what is the purpose of our existence? The Bible addresses the origin of existence in its opening statement, "In the beginning God created the heavens and the earth" (Gen. 1:1). The first issue the early church fathers dealt with regarding creation was this: Is creation an extension of God or a direct act bringing into being something other than God?

The answer to this question is fundamental to the entire Christian view of salvation. Certain fathers, notably Origen, whose views were rejected by the church, argued that creation is an extension of God. After much debate the fathers answered that God and creation have "separate and totally dissimilar modes of existence."[11] Creation is not an extension of God. Instead, God created the world *ex nihilio*, out of nothing. Christians have never identified the natural world as God. Creation, the fathers affirmed, is a result of an act of God's will. God called into being a created essence, a reality other than himself. Saint Gregory of Nazianzen speaks the Christian view: "There is an infinite distance between God and creation, and this is a distance of natures. All is distant from God, and is remote from him not by place, but by nature."[12]

This view is expressed in the first article of the Apostles' Creed, "I believe in God the Father Almighty, Creator of heaven and earth." The created order does not participate in the essence of the Creator. It is a substance and a reality that is altogether different.

Why is it important for us to embrace this ancient interpretation in our postmodern world? It is because today's postmodern popular spirituality is based on the ancient heresy that the world of nature is an extension of God. This issue needs to be understood in the historical framework of the twentieth century as we seek to make disciples of Jesus.

The primary spiritual conflict during most of the twentieth century was between Christianity and secularism. Secularism argued against all views of the supernatural, insisting that science and reason had conclusively demonstrated that material existence is all there is. Secularism led to everything from an existential individualism that urged people to "create your own meaning" to a government-controlled communist world that promised economic equality and justice for all in a yet-to-come golden era. Salvation, secularism proclaims, does not come from the outside; it comes from the inside—from your internal self or from government control.

Then came the sixties revolution. It opened the West to the Eastern world and its philosophies and religions. Through the East, an alternative view to both Christianity and secularism emerged. It introduced a new spirituality into culture. This spirituality is based on the ancient notion that God and nature are one. This view has influenced every area of life—ecology, health, business, science, the arts, history, values, and education as well as matters dealing with creation, evil, redemption, and the future life. It is called New Age spirituality.

This New Age view of creation is articulated by Shirley MacLaine. She has said, "If everyone was taught one basic spiritual law, your world would be a happier, healthier place, and that law is: Everyone is God, everyone."[13] MacLaine articulates the ancient philosophy of monism: "All is one." This post-Christian New Age spirituality makes no distinction between God and nature, God and persons, God and reality—all is one undifferentiated and interconnected energy. This "oneness of everything" must be taken into account as we proclaim the mission of God in today's world. Obviously if God and nature are one, there can be no saving mission of God to the world. Instead each of us has as our own mission to discover the God or the Christ who is within (a New Age philosophy).

In today's world it is imperative that disciples understand the fundamental difference between the prevalent New Age spirituality and the Christian understanding of spirituality. New Age proponents use a language of spirituality that is strikingly similar to the language of Christianity. They speak of prayer, meditation, relationship with God, and discovering Christ. But in the end all this language has to do with "getting in touch with the God who is within me."

Christian language differs from New Age language, and the difference starts with the issue of creation. Creation is not God, and God is not the creation. God created the world out of nothing, and it is of a different essence. God sustains the creation by the Spirit. God was united with the creation in the incarnation. Because Jesus was a sacrifice for our sins and won a victory over the powers of evil, a relationship with creatures and creation has been restored. Thus, we have faith, not in ourselves, but in Jesus Christ through whom we have a relationship with God. (New Age conversion and spirituality is self-actualized.)

One area where common cause may be made with New Age proponents is in the understanding that all of life is interrelated. While Christians affirm the distinction between God and creation, we can and do affirm the interconnection of all things *within* the created order. Creation is not a conglomeration of unrelated parts but more like a web of interrelated connections. While Christians may connect with the new concern for the unity of all creation, Christians vigorously uphold the ancient interpretation that God created, by his will, a created order that is outside of himself yet dependent and contingent upon him. God is not absent from his creation nor indifferent to it. He loves the entire creation—all of nature, which reflects his creativity, and all of humanity, made in his image. Because "God so loved the world" he *sent* his Son to reclaim creatures and creation to himself. Thus conversion and spirituality come from *outside* creation and the self, not from the inside of human consciousness.

Creation Is Good

The biblical claim that God's mission is to recover both creatures and creation affirms creation as good. The issue regarding creation in the early church was over the nature of materiality. Is the material order good or evil? This question, like that of the origin of creation, is crucial to an understanding of God's mission.

The second-century Gnostic perversion of Christianity argued that material reality was evil. They posited an eternal conflict between good and evil, a conflict that reached back into eternal past. Gnostics taught that an eternal spirit was the source of all good and an eternal material god was the source of all evil. The material god, they believed, was the creator. Consequently matter was evil. On the other hand they argued that all souls came from the spirit god and were good. They believed humans were a mixture of the material reality, which was evil, and the eternal spiritual reality, which was good. Consequently the problem of the human condition was that every person had a *good soul imprisoned in an evil, material body*. The Gnostics' goal of salvation was to free the soul from its imprisonment to the body. This was accomplished, they taught, by an "enlightenment" that came from Jesus. Jesus had been sent by the pure spirit god as a phantom (he did not have a real body, otherwise he would have had the same problem as all other persons) to deliver the knowledge that would enlighten people and set them free. The knowledge he communicated was simply that the spirit within did not have to be subject to the body.

The early church fathers were united in their conviction that there is only one God, that this God is the Creator, and that creation is good. In response to the Gnostics, the fathers of the church wrote creedal statements that affirmed the goodness of creation. These statements, called "the rule of faith," were the earliest version of the Apostles' Creed.[14] Essentially, the "rule of faith" emphasizes three reasons why creation is good: God made creation; God became the creation in the incarnation; God will restore the creation at the end of history.

Why is it essential for us to make disciples who embrace the goodness of creation? Because it speaks a necessary antidote to the incipient Gnosticism that continues to lurk in some churches even today. For example, when the salvation of the body is rejected, the inadvertent assumption is that the soul is eternal but the body is perishable. This erroneous conviction results in a privatistic view of salvation. "After all, if the soul is eternal and the body is temporal, and if we really catch the full significance of this difference, what possible value could our world, our history, and our bodies have, apart from being merely a testing ground or a ticket station for what is truly important, eternal and valuable?"[15] This view is also very similar to a New Age refrain that is often stated this way, "The real me is the spirit that is within. I need to get in touch with this spirit, to release it to find the God that lives within me." This is a popular New Age view of salvation, one that was refuted by ancient Christianity.

Biblically, salvation and Christian discipleship is not a release from the material world. Rather salvation is a release from a life lived in obedience to the powers of evil. True salvation and Christian discipleship is an obedience to Christ that results in a new life lived in this world. Yes, of course there is a world to come. But first we are called to live under God in this material world, in its structures of relationships—family, political, economic, and social realities—in a redemptive way. An *otherworldly* Christianity that seeks to escape from this world produces Gnostics who fail to demonstrate how a Christian witness affirms life in this world as a good gift of the Creator. Furthermore, the teaching that God's mission is to the whole world affirms the unity between the spiritual and material. It confesses that God's intention is to rescue the whole created order, as Paul himself states, "The creation itself will be liberated from its bondage to decay and brought into the glorious freedom of the children of God" (Rom. 8:21).

Made for Relationship

The apex of God's creation is humanity made in God's image and likeness (Gen. 1:26). By nature human beings are different from God (not an extension of God as New Age spirituality teaches). Men and women have been made to be in fellowship with God, to be in communion with their Creator. The early church fathers taught that God made humans as "open beings," called to grow in relationship with God. The concept of "likeness" suggests "the idea of dynamic progress and implies human freedom" according to the Greek fathers.[16] This implies that God is known in relationship and through the experience of communion as opposed to the more Western notion that makes God known primarily through the intellect. "A true Christian knows God through a free and conscious experience; this is precisely the friendship with God that was man's state before the fall—the state in which God wanted man to live and was restored in Jesus Christ."[17]

Men and women were not only given the calling to be in communion with God but were also called to the task of caring for God's creation. The Reformed community calls this the cultural mandate. Thus Adam and Eve are told that they are "to work" and to "take care" of the Garden of Eden (Gen. 2:15). This is Christian vocation, the subject of the last stage and, clearly, a dimension of Christian formation.

The assignment to be culturally engaged demonstrates the unity between spirit and body and the unity of the person's relationship with God. Through the Spirit we enter into communion with God, and in obedience to God we are to care for God's world, to unfold its riches, and to serve God in the structure of life itself. Yet our relationship with God, our service to God in this life has become corrupted through sin. Because of sin, the image of God in us is marred and the work we do has become distorted. (This is why Christian formation must include an understanding of Christian vocation.) Christians bear the restored image; thus all their work is in the service of God.

The Problem of Evil

Evil arises from freedom and is throughout Scripture understood as the choice to rebel against God. The disobedience of God's creatures—first the angels and then Adam and Eve seduced by the fallen Lucifer—is the source of evil. Because all creatures are in Adam, we all inherit from Adam this nature of disobedience, and like him, all disobey God and become subject to death (Rom. 5:12).

The fathers of the church follow this same line of thinking. Justin Martyr wrote, "God, when He had made the whole world, and subjected things early to man . . . committed the care of men and of all things under heaven to angels [who] transgressed this appointment."[18] Irenaeus wrote that Satan "apostatized from God of his own free-will."[19] Satan then tempted Adam and Eve and caused them to rebel against God of their own free choice. Tatian, understanding our freedom this way, interpreted Genesis 3:1 to mean that "through their freedom of choice [they] have been given up to their own infatuation."[20] For Tatian and the early church fathers in general, "the tragic nature of the world in its present condition is the result of angels and humans misusing their free will."[21]

The meaning of evil is clear: It is "a radical opposition to God, a revolt, a disobedience, a resistance."[22] This war on God is traceable to the fall of Lucifer in the heavens and to humans on earth. It is a force, a violent energy, and an active design against God. Thus God himself is engaged in a struggle with these powers of darkness.

God's struggle is not with the material creation. God made the world good. God's war is against the principalities and the powers. These powers have defaced the image of God in humans. Instead of being in a loving relationship with God, we rebel against God and his purposes in the world.

God is at war with those principalities and powers of evil that capture the minds and hearts of God's creatures and lead them, through the choices they make, to do evil in God's creation. It is this choice to do evil that has resulted in a world full of evil. Evil is never seen as a material substance. It is, instead, an opposition to God's will. The fall is therefore not "an erroneous choice, not just an option for the wrong direction, but rather a refusal to ascend toward God, a desertion from the service of God."[23] For Adam and Eve the choice was not between good and evil, for they had no understanding of evil. Instead their choice was between obedience to God or a turning into themselves. According to Athanasius, "The human fall consists precisely in the fact that man limits himself to himself, that man becomes, as it were, in love with himself."[24] Because Adam and Eve concentrated on themselves, their needs, their interests, and their desires instead of God's calling to be in relationship with him, they despiritualized human existence. They opened their own lives, the lives of their descendants, and the life of the whole world to self-interest and self-love. Their choice was "more profound even than a false choice of direction." Rather, "it was the infidelity of love, the insane separation from the Only One who is worthy of affection and love" that now "envelops all creatures and the entire cosmos."[25] All of humanity has chosen to live as servants of unrighteousness, choosing the fatal attraction to evil that destroys their relation to God and to the doing of his work in the world. The penalty for this sin is death—physical death and an eternal separation from God, the only true source of life.

How can this sorry situation be reversed? What can God do to restore man's and woman's relationship with himself and restore their task to serve God through his work and worship in this world? God's task, the reversal of the human situation and with it the renewal of relationship, human vocation, and the gift of eternal life, is the *Missio Dei* accomplished by the incarnation, death, resurrection, and coming again of Jesus.

The recapitulation was accomplished by God the Creator, who sent his Son to do for us what we are not able to do for ourselves. We cannot rescue ourselves from the plight of evil. We cannot save ourselves. We cannot restore our relationship with God. We cannot restore the image of God in which we are created. The sin of the first man, Adam, plunged us into a violent, deliberate disobedience to our Creator. Only God can save us. God "became flesh." By the complete obedience of Jesus to the Father and by his sacrifice for sin, he won a decisive victory over the powers of evil. At the end of history his victory will be completely accomplished in the final judgment against evil and in the formation of the new heavens and earth. The end of the world and the eternal future is known only through Jesus. The story of God's mission to the world is not complete without an understanding of how God in Christ restores and recapitulates the world of creatures and creation to himself in the eschatological redemption and re-creation of all things. We turn then from the problem of evil that permeates life and affects the created order to the consummation of God's mission at the end of history.

Redemption, Eschatology, and Re-creation

It is my experience that some Christians do not believe that the work of Christ extends to the entire creation. When I discuss this matter with some, the response is often an adamant, "I don't believe it!" This response, of course, is a reflection of our individualistic, rationalistic, and nonembodied modern view of Christianity. This nonbiblical view holds that salvation is to individuals, not to the whole earth. It also often teaches salvation is the soul only, not the whole person.[26]

This nonphysical view of the faith bears some similarity to the Gnostic rejection of the flesh in the second century. Nevertheless, I don't know of a true Christian who would reject the idea that God created the world. Nor do I know of a Christian who would deny that God's incarnation in Jesus Christ is a real incarnation into the flesh of humanity and a real life in a particular time, place, and history. Contemporary Christians are not Gnostics. Most have simply not thought through the entire biblical message.

However, the manner in which some present the way of salvation often bears similarities to aspects of the Gnostic message. The downside of this truncated message is that it leaves new disciples open to the falsehood of New Age convictions. For example, salvation is sometimes presented as *otherworldly*. It is as though there is something wrong with having a body and living in this world. In this view, to believe in Jesus is to gain an ultimate release from this body so that one may enjoy the eternal salvation of the soul. To teach this is to deny the resurrection of the body.

The view that separates the soul from the body is not only a nonbiblical view of redemption, it also results in an incorrect view of what it means to be a disciple and what it means to be a spiritual person. The Christian life is cast into a negative role and is defined by what a person does not do. It fails to understand our work in the world as a response of discipleship. For this reason it is imperative to grasp the physical side of being spiritual. Spirituality is not a release from the physical nor a condemnation of the physical. Instead, it is a redemption, a renewing and restoring of the physical. Consequently the eschatological vision of God's mission is not the destruction of all that is physical so that the spiritual may exist throughout eternity unencumbered by the physical. No, the eschatological vision is that the face of God's earth will be renewed, that all that is death will be done away with, put away forever, so that all that is life will endure forever.

Neither the Bible nor the early church fathers speculate on the nature of the redeemed world, the eschatological re-creation of all things. But there are several convictions that regulate our vision of the future. First, the Pauline testimony and that of the early church fathers is that the creation will be *liberated from its bondage to decay.* The fathers see this as a kind of transfiguration of creation. The powers of evil will be destroyed. These powers will no longer be able to seduce humanity and to do evil through the structures of existence. Creation will be released, renovated, restored, and made whole. This transfiguration will occur as an act of God upon creation. It is his work of transfiguration, his work of destroying the powers and of releasing creation from the unrelenting influence of evil. What this means precisely we dare not say. It is a mystery within God's sovereignty. Yet this we know: the new creation is the hope we have in this world (Rom. 8: 18–22). The redemption of humanity, however, is of another sort. Not all of humanity will be redeemed. Because God made us in his image with the gift of choice, humanity will be judged, but "whoever believes in him" will be saved (John 3:16). Regardless of how *whoever* is interpreted, not all will be saved. Calvinists believe that God turns the heart of the elect to embrace Jesus in faith. Arminians stress the universal offer of salvation recognizing that not all will embrace Jesus. Others believe a final offer of salvation will be made on the day of judgment. In spite of these differences, all agree that not all will be saved. Those who for one reason or another do not embrace God's grace and eternal life have chosen for themselves eternal death—an eternal separation from God, the giver of life.

What we do know for sure is that at the end of history as we know it, God will put away evil forever, every knee will bow and confess Jesus as Lord, and there will be a new heaven and a new earth in which God will reign forever. In view of this cosmic message, salvation extends to the end of the earth. The message of the church is, "Whoever is thirsty, let him come; and whoever wishes, let him take the free gift of the water of life" (Rev. 22:17).

Death is vanquished. Life endures forever! New Christians are formed in this message of hope.

Conclusion

I have attempted to summarize God's mission to the world. This is where the content of our evangelism, discipleship, and Christian formation must start. It is the Good News, the message in which we are to be formed. Because this news must take root in a world characterized by New Age spirituality, it is imperative for us to form new Christians who grasp the fullness of God's mission—the salvation of creatures and creation.

God has created a world that is wholly other than himself. God made humans in his image and after his likeness and gave them the task to take care of his world under his authority. Yet humans, influenced by the powers of evil that rebelled against God, have sinned and revolted against God. Because of sin, humans have been condemned to death, a death that expresses itself not only in physical death but also in the failure to unfold creation according to the will of God. Consequently, our work in the world expresses our fallen nature and has produced estrangement, not only between humans and God but between humans and God's creation.

God's mission from the very beginning has been to restore communion with his creatures and creation. The story of Israel and Jesus unravel God's mission. God becomes involved in our history to restore a relationship with us and with the world. God becomes incarnate, and as the second Adam, he does for us what we cannot do for ourselves. In Jesus Christ God is united with our humanity. Because of his love for us, he recapitulates the work of the first Adam. He lives a perfect life for us. He is a sacrifice for our sin. He conquers death on the cross. By his resurrection he restores life to us and gives us the promise of a new heaven and a new earth where sin and death will be no more. Now he calls us to live together in the community of his name, the church—that special people who by their very existence and by their worship witness to the work of God's redeeming grace. Here, in this community and in its worship, evangelism occurs, disciples are made, spiritual formation is accomplished, and a person's place and work in this world find true meaning. This is what it means to make disciples in a post-Christian world.

Table 17: The Mission of God in Jesus Christ

Theme	Comments
The mission of Jesus according to the biblical writers	The mission of God is to rescue the world through the work of Jesus. He bound Satan; he was a sacrifice for sin; he was Victor over the powers of evil; he showed us how to live.
The mission of Jesus according to the early church fathers	The *recapitulation* of all things. He reverses what Adam did to creatures and creation and provides salvation for creatures and creation.

Table 18: Creation and the Fall

Theme	Comments
Creation	Creation is *not* an extension of God. Creation is of a different essence than God but wholly dependent upon God, who sustains it by the word of his power.
Creation is Good	Spirituality is not an escape from creation as New Age spirituality teaches. Christian spirituality affirms the unity of body and soul. Biblical Christianity is holistic.
Made for relationship	God is known in relationship.
The problem of evil	Evil is a radical opposition to God, a revolt, a disobedience (first by the angels, then by humans). The problem is sin; the result is death.
God's mission accomplished in the eschaton	Because of the work of Jesus, the face of God's earth will be renewed. Both creatures and creation will be released from the influence and impact of the evil powers. The new heavens and the new earth will endure.

Questions for Discussion

1. What is the mission of God?
2. How has Jesus accomplished the mission of God?
3. Why is it important for discipleship and spirituality to affirm the goodness of God's creation?
4. If evil is "a radical opposition to God, a revolt, a disobedience, a resistance," what then is conversion, discipleship, spirituality, and Christian vocation? Develop this thoroughly as you think through how you will form new Christians in each area.
   - What is conversion?
   - What is discipleship?
   - What is spirituality?
   - What is Christian vocation?

9

THE CHURCH
THAT TELLS THE STORY

If the mission of God through Jesus Christ is to rescue creation from the presence and power of evil, then what is the mission of the church? If the church is the context for Christian formation, we must then have a biblical view of the purpose of the church. There seems to be some confusion about the purpose of the church in both the mainline and evangelical communities. Let me explain.

Back in 1979 a church leader sent a letter to evangelical leaders declaring, "God is calling us to march into the halls of Congress and clean up America for God." His concerns were certainly appropriate: the rise of the permissive society, the breakdown of marriage, violence in the streets, pornography, abortion, and drugs to name a few issues that pointed to the breakdown of American society. Rev. Jerry Falwell's answer was to found the Moral Majority and through this organization mobilize churches throughout America to vote Christians into office. These Christians were to act as responsible moral citizens in places of power. The idea was that through them a reforming and stable influence would be established to stem the eroding values of a godless American culture. The particular arm of the government through which evangelicals were to fulfill their calling to be salt and light to the world was the Republican Party.

In the meantime the mainline church was also mobilizing to assert an influence on another set of political problems—poverty, racism, the crumbling of the inner city, gangs, and the meaninglessness found among the jobless, single mothers, and aging dependents. For mainliners, these matters of raising humanity to a more humane level was the goal of the church, and the arm of the government through which this task was to be accomplished was the Democratic Party.[1]

What's wrong with this picture then and now? The church was being politicized. That is, this view says the agenda of the church is accomplished by teaming with a political power of the world. This view compromises the purposes of the church. It results in a distortion of the church's mission to the world. Yet this view persists. Consequently we must ask: What is the purpose and mission of the church?

The mission of the church is most succinctly expressed in Ephesians 3:10, "His intent was that now, through the church, the manifold wisdom of God should be made known to the rulers and authorities in the heavenly realms." This mission of the church needs to be understood in the context of Paul's prayer for the church in Ephesians 1:15–23. The vision of the prayer is that of Christ and his eschatological reign over all things. Paul understands the mission of the church to witness to Jesus as Lord and to call people into repentance, faith, obedience, and hope.

The mission of the church is not to accomplish God's eschatological reign. The church does not bring in the kingdom. It does not establish God's reign over society. God has already accomplished his goals for humanity and for the cosmos in Jesus Christ. The church in this period of history between the cross and the return of Christ witnesses to an accomplished fact. It witnesses to the reign of Jesus Christ over all creation and lives in the hope of its final realization in the second coming of Jesus Christ.

The mission of the church is to be about the politics of Jesus. Jesus is Lord. He has won a victory over the powers of evil and is now and shall forever be the reigning Lord over everything God has created. The church is called to live this truth, proclaim it, enact it, and call people to a saving knowledge of Jesus Christ and to a life of obedient discipleship under his reign in their lives.[2]

In this chapter, I will develop this mission of the church under two headings: the theological basis for the mission of the church, and witnessing to God's mission in a post-Christian world. How the church views its mission will influence its approach to Christian formation.

The Theological Basis for the Mission of the Church

In God's divine providence, he has created a people to witness to his existence, to his active presence in the world, to his saving work, and to his eschatological reign over all creation. This people, the church, arises from the triune God and especially the work of the Holy Spirit.

The Church Arises from the Spirit

I have already made reference to the trinitarian activity of God in the world. The Father sends the Son, the Father and the Son send the Spirit, the Spirit sends the church and dwells within it.[3] Paul places the sending of the Son and the sending of the Spirit side by side. "God sent his Son . . . to redeem those under the law. . . . Because you are sons, God sent the Spirit of his Son into our hearts. . . . Since you are a son, God has also made you an heir" (Gal. 4:4–7). Paul brings together the sending of the Son and the Spirit, who together bring forth the church.

This passage states two very important truths about the church—truths that are imperative to keep in mind as we think about the mission of the church to make disciples to live under the lordship of Christ. First, in the church we are dealing with God himself. The church is not a mere collection of individuals, a human entity, but in a mystical way it is a real and actual experience that connects with the Son and the Spirit. If this is true, then the life of the church itself plays a crucial role in evangelism. Evangelism will occur not only through the words the church delivers but through the way the words are embodied and lived out by the church.

Second, if the Spirit truly creates the church, then the church is by the power of the Spirit brought into the dynamic fellowship of the triune God. This vision of the church participating in the life of God directly impacts our understanding of Christian formation and spirituality. Spirituality will be realized primarily in community. True Christianity occurs in a discipleship with others joined in communion with the triune God.

This dynamic of the church participating in the triune God by the Spirit points to the church as the people of God's presence. The church is the habitation of God's dwelling in the world, the instrument of God's voice to witness to God's mission for the world. Here among these people is a people where the lost can be in touch with God's provision for them in Jesus Christ. Here God's vision for their relationships, values, and vocation are learned. Unfortunately, many congregations do not function with this supernatural conviction of the church. Voicing his concern over the church losing its mission, one pastor wrote, "I have grown disillusioned with the church. . . . Let's forget attendance, forget growth, forget revivals, forget outreach programs, forget all the quantitative elements of the consumer culture and focus on the church living out the mission of God in daily living. . . . Let's go to those whose lives are in such disarray that they recognize their need for a lifestyle conversion. . . . I have found that the outcasts are more open and more willing to hear and do all that is required for genuine conversion . . . conversion must be a process in which the seeker is held accountable, not just for doctrine, but lifestyle."[4]

Perhaps many of today's Western churches are too respectable, too sophisticated, too rich, too powerful, too self-sufficient, too proud, and too comfortable to let down their defenses and become authentic communities created by the Spirit living in communal fellowship with the triune God. Darrell Harris, chaplain of the Institute for Worship Studies, says we should "pray for the Holy Spirit to do a ruinous work among us."[5] Perhaps our churches will not experience the presence and the power of the Spirit until our churchy clubs and business-driven models are brought to ruin. Scary thought. Are we blocking the work of the Spirit by our easy believism and culturally defined churches?

Perhaps we need to recover the christological nature of the church. What does it means to say that the nature of the church is christological? Theological thinking allows that just as Jesus is fully divine and fully human, so also the church's mission to the world needs to be seen in terms of its divine calling and human manifestation.

The church lives in a sense "before God" and "before the world." We need to see the church's mission to the world from these two aspects.

The Divine Calling of the Church

In the previous chapter I have identified God's mission as it extends from creation and the fall to the redeeming work of Christ and the ultimate recapitulation of all things. The divine mission of the church is to be a witness to God's purposes accomplished in history. Consequently the church calls on people to believe in Jesus and to live under his reign in the community of the church. The biblical images of the church help us understand more clearly this divine nature of the church.

To begin, it seems helpful to recall that the church serves a mission similar to that of Israel prior to the coming of God's Son into the world. Peter writes the defining comparison, "You are a chosen people, a royal priesthood, a holy nation, a people belonging to God, that you may declare the praises of him who called you out of darkness into his wonderful light" (1 Peter 2:9). This is the same way the writer of Deuteronomy describes Israel's calling in the world (e.g., 7:6, 14:2, 26:18). The church, like Israel, has a divine origin and calling. This divine nature of the church is caught in the New Testament images of the church, especially the church as the people of God, the new creation, the fellowship in faith, and the body of Christ. These images speak of a people who are united in a new kind of bond and relationship that transcends barriers of rich and poor, male and female, black, white, yellow, or red. This community is so different and unusual that it can be called the "body of Christ." Getting in touch with this community in its most ideal sense is getting in touch with the very life of God.

The Church as a Human Manifestation of God's Mission

The church is also God's people in a particular time in history and at a specific geographical place. The church is always the church in Asia, Africa, Europe, Latin America, North America, or in one of the many cultures of the world. For this reason, the divine mission of the church must be contextualized. While the church's witness to the mission of God never changes, the particular way it expresses its mission will change from place to place. While God's church is one and is directed to every people group and nation, its external appearance will reflect the cultural situation in which its ministry occurs. One group of people may meet in a cathedral, another in a modest rural church, another in a warehouse. While the divine nature and calling of the people who comprise the church remains the same, the style will differ from place to place and culture to culture.

Today's postmodern culture is forcing the church to move out of its association with the model of the church that was developed in the Christian era. Consider the following comparisons between the church in the Christian era and the church in the present, post-Christian era.

In the Christian era, existing in one form or another from the time of Constantine to the recent past, the church has functioned primarily as the place for personal private devotion and individual faith and relationship with God. Also, due to the church's symbiotic relationship to "Christian culture," the church has served the culture as its "chaplain." Prayer at public events and preaching serve as the culture's moral conscience. Furthermore, the teaching of the church supports good morals and communicates the ethic by which society is to live. The resources of the church such as its worship, Scripture, and various programs for children and adults assist people to live good, moral, and upright lives. The clergy provide religious goods such as moral teaching, baptisms, confirmations, marriages, and funerals, and the people consume these goods. Then the laypeople who work in the world in various structures of existence contribute to the welfare of society by living as good, upright citizens modeling the good life for others and teaching people how to live decent, law-abiding lives.

157

However, the church of the post-Christian era is more like the church of the first three centuries. It is similar to the church to which 1 Peter was written—a countercultural community. Peter refers to these people as "aliens and strangers in the world." He urges them to "abstain from sinful desires" and "live such good lives among the pagans that, though they accuse you of doing wrong, they may see your good deeds and glorify God" (1 Peter 2:11–12). The post-Christian church does not serve a political party or seek to legislate Christian morality on society. Instead its purpose is to become the embodied reality of the rule of Christ over the lives of its people. It fosters an alternative way of life in the world. This new paradigm is a community of people living out of a different vision of life and a different ethic. The values by which people live within this community are the values of the kingdom. They live in harmony with each other, supporting one another, caring for each other's needs, looking out for each other. They witness within society by acting toward their neighbors and functioning at work by the same values.

In brief, the model of the church in the Christian era looks more like the culture because culture is being impacted by Christian values. However, as the idea of a Christian society has broken down and as society has become less and less formed by Christian principles, the distance between society and the church has become greater.

In this situation, many contemporary church leaders argue that the most effective churches will be those that allow Christian commitments to connect with the more laissez-faire attitudes of society. By making Christianity more like the culture of which it is a part, some argue, the church becomes more attractive, more relevant, and more accessible. This kind of church, it is proclaimed, will grow and have the greatest impact on our post-Christian culture.

On the other hand, the missional church argues for an opposite view. In a post-Christian society the church needs to be an alternative culture. It needs to be defined over against the ruling values of society. Like the early church, the church today is a pilgrim church in an alien and foreign land. The culture of the world in which we live is so thoroughly shaped by the principalities and the powers that the church must become a sign, a foretaste, and a witness to a humanity and a world shaped by the vision of God's reign over the lives of his people. This alternative culture is not just an individual here and there willing to live a life of radical discipleship, but it is local communities of people who gather to be church together. It is these people, these communities of faith that will evangelize, disciple, and form Christians in a post-Christian world. These people, formed as Christians who live countercultural lifestyles, are the ones who will make the greatest impact on society.

Witnessing to God's Mission in a Post-Christian World

The church, which is the presence of divine life in the world, must concretize its divine life in human form. What does it take to do this? The New Testament and early church tradition point to at least two ways that the church expresses its divine mission within the world: It is called to be an *otherworldly* community and a people who proclaim and enact God's vision of the world in worship.

Called to Be an Otherworldly Community

First, the church that would be an effective evangelizing and discipling church in the post-Christian world is called to be an *otherworldly* community. The church is (1) *called,* (2) a *community,* and (3) *otherworldly.*

The church is called. No one can deny the nature of the church as a called community. In his letter to the Ephesian church, Paul puts the church's calling this way: "For he chose us in him before the creation of the world to be holy and blameless in his sight" (Eph. 1:4). "In him we were also chosen, having been predestined according to the plan of him who works out everything in conformity with the purpose of his will" (Eph. 1:11). While exegetes from different traditions may interpret these verses either in terms of foreordination or foreknowledge, all agree that they point to the church as a people who are called into existence by God for a specific purpose.

The church is called to be a community. After declaring how they were once dead in their transgressions and sins, Paul turns to their new state, that of community. He says, "You are . . . fellow citizens with God's people and members of God's household" (Eph. 2:19).

The church is called to be an otherworldly community. Throughout the Book of Ephesians Paul also clearly and repeatedly states that these people, the church at Ephesus, have an otherworldly perspective.* He contrasts their former life with their present life when he says, "You followed the ways of this world and of the ruler of the kingdom of the air, the spirit who is now at work in those who are disobedient. . . . [But God] made us alive with Christ . . . and seated us with him in the heavenly realms in Christ Jesus" (Eph. 2:2, 5–6).

This understanding of the church is the resurrection of the ancient apologetic. God is not a mere theoretical idea or abstract creator and ruler of the universe known through intellectual syllogisms or arguments.

Otherworldly does not mean the church rejects God's creation and its place in it. It means it is ruled and shaped by the values of God's kingdom as it lives in this world.

Rather, God who was incarnated in Jesus for our sake continues to have a presence in the world. Jesus is found in the flesh and blood of those who gather in his name to proclaim his greatness and to live transformed lives together.

What does this add up to? It means that there is a people in the world with a particular message, the Good News of God's mission to the world. It means that these people who have been transformed by this message have a particular interpretation of the world because they see it from creation to re-creation through the eyes of God's mission. It means that these people also have a very specific experience of the world because they see it through the eyes of its eschatological redemption.

In the post-Christian, postmodern world in which we live, the most crucial witness to the world is a vital, Spirit-filled local church that is animated by the message of God's mission. Nothing is more important for evangelism and discipleship than a community of people who have been evangelized by the message of God's mission to the world and who, through a deep commitment to God and each other, seek to live out their lives in obedience to God.

Because I travel a great deal, I have the opportunity to visit many churches. I generally catch the spirit of a church quickly. In some churches I get the sense that people are there out of duty and habit. I experience no incentive to return or to become involved in this kind of church. In other churches I sense joy, an electric feeling of "I want to be here." I can sense the difference between the two types of churches. The latter church is animated by the Good News, by a sense of being the community of God, by a sense of knowing who we are, what this world is all about, and what our place is in the world.

The church that wants to become an evangelizing and discipling community will have to become a people who are animated by the message of God. They need to show that they are a people in whom the very life of God is manifested.

As mentioned in chapter 4, Cyprian of Carthage in the middle of the third century expressed the ancient church's divine self-understanding. "You cannot have God for your father if you have not the church for your mother."[6] The church is the womb in which we are conceived and brought forth. The only womb that brings forth life is the womb that has life. Consequently, the process of evangelism and discipleship requires a church to be animated by the life of God.

The first responsibility of the congregation that is committed to making disciples in the post-Christian world is to be an alternative community of people who see and live life differently.

Proclaiming and Enacting God's Vision of the World in Worship

As noted already, the church that would be an evangelizing and discipling church must pay attention to its worship. It is interesting that when the church is addressed as a community, the New Testament writer almost always adds a comment about the church at worship. This is the case in the Ephesians context mentioned above. For example, our predestination in Christ is "to the praise of his glorious grace" (Eph. 1:6) and "in order that we, who were the first to hope in Christ, might be for the praise of his glory" (Eph. 1:12). In this same passage Paul refers to the cosmic scope of God's saving mission, which is the subject of our worship. Referring to the death and resurrection of Jesus, Paul strikes at the theme of Christian worship: "I pray . . . that you may know the hope to which he has called you, the riches of his glorious inheritance in the saints, and his incomparably great power for us who believe. That power is like the working of his mighty strength, which he exerted in Christ when he raised him from the dead and seated him at his right hand in the heavenly realms, far above all rule and authority, power and dominion, and every title that can be given, not only in the present age but also in the one to come. And God placed all things under his feet and appointed him to be head over everything for the church, which is his body, the fullness of him who fills everything in every way" (Eph. 1:18–23).

This passage is clear. Worship is not about *me* and *my experience;* it is about God and God's mission to save humanity and to rescue the world through Jesus Christ's death, resurrection, and coming again. Worship is both remembrance *(anamnesis)* and anticipation *(prolepsis)*. It has to do with the praise of God for God's mission to the world in the past, in the present, and in the future.[7]

It is interesting that people who are experts in the area of worship seldom connect worship with mission, and people who are experts in mission seldom connect mission with worship. The mission of the church to make disciples occurs in worship. The two go hand in hand. God's mission is proclaimed and enacted in the worship of God's earthly community, the church, which embodies God's mission. Worship and mission are not separate categories of ministry but interrelated aspects of the one single ministry of declaring God's saving mission and of bringing people into an experience of God's salvation in a special body of people, the church.

Worship is first and foremost the mission of God proclaimed and enacted. All of worship, the gathering of God's people—the preached Word, the thanksgiving at bread and wine, the sending forth—all of it is God's mission. Likewise, everything the congregation does in these four movements is mission—the singing, praying, collection, Scripture reading, use of the arts, the going forth into the world—all of it is mission.

This kind of worship is *upward* because it offers praise to God for his mission in creating and redeeming the world. It is *inward* because it shapes each of us in God's community to reflect on the world from the perspective of God's saving mission and to bring our own lives into conformity to the living out of the kingdom principles that give shape to God's kingdom community. It is *outward* in that it proclaims God's mission to the watching world and provides them with an alternative view of reality. In this sense worship *is* the mission of God and *does* the mission of God and *calls* us all into submission and obedience to the God of the mission. This kind of worship evangelizes, disciples, spiritually forms, and manifests Christian vocation because it is God oriented in its thanksgiving, private and personal in its impact on the worshiper, and public in its interpretation of the world and its history.

It is this kind of worship that will engage the post-Christian world. First, the post-Christian world has no true center; much of its popular New Age spirituality makes the human individual the center of the universe. We are urged to find the meaning of the world and even the presence of the divine within our own being. Yet in true worship, in preaching, at the table, and in song Christ is celebrated at the center. Through him the entire world from its beginning to its ending is understood. Worship preaches and enacts the overthrow of the powers of evil so that people defined by sin, concerned over terror, enslaved by poverty, and distraught over the needs of the world see a new reality proclaimed by worship and embodied by the worshiping community.

Second, in worship one should experience an alternative to the three great problems of our current existence in the world—isolationism, individualism, and consumerism. Worship that focuses on Jesus Christ, who freely gave his life that others may live, points to the fulfillment of life through a self-giving that overcomes the loneliness of isolationism. Worship addresses our individualism as it points to our belonging to a community of God's people throughout history, around the world, and actualized in this community of local believers. Worship also points away from consumerism as the source of meaning as it focuses on the meaning found in Jesus Christ and a life lived in obedience to him that gives to others.[8]

Third, worship expresses hope for the future. In a world made vulnerable by terrorism, in a world in which the notion of progress toward a golden future of the world has been smashed, in a world of uncertainty and fear, worship enacts hope. Worship says the outcome of the world is certain and hopeful. The world is not simply a chaotic mess left to the whims of its leaders. God has a plan, an outcome for the world that is certain. In the midst of the insecurities of life, there is hope.

There is in this world a witness to the mission of God. It is found in the church, which by its very existence is an embodiment of God's mission. Because of the church, the world may know that there is a God and that God is at work in the world now calling a people to himself. This people, in their worship, "declare the praises of him who called you out of darkness into his wonderful light" (1 Peter 2:9). The church at worship is the mission of God made public.

Conclusion

I have attempted to show throughout this book that the church has clearly entered into a new phase of history—the post-Christian era. I have also attempted to make it clear that the surrounding culture in which the church finds itself in North America and around the world no longer supports the claims of the gospel. I have also insinuated, without being obvious about it, that the general tenor of Christian faith has been watered down to a view perilously close to the *meism* and experience-centered popular spirituality of the day. In this setting the very substance of the gospel—both its doctrine and lifestyle—are threatened.

For these reasons there is a need to recover key elements of the gospel: the *substance* of God's mission, the *community* that embodies God's mission, and the *worship* that proclaims and enacts it. In addition to these three realities there is one more, and that has been the main subject of this book: *how new Christians are formed into disciples of Jesus.* The church is called, as the International Consultation on Discipleship has clearly stated, not only to bring the unchurched to the point of conversion but to establish a process to make lifelong disciples of Jesus, the Savior of the world and the Master of our lives.

Table 19: The Theological Basis for the Mission of the Church

Theme	Comments
The church arises from the Spirit	The church, created by the Spirit, participates in the life of the triune God. Evangelism occurs not only through the words the church speaks but also, and perhaps especially, through the *life* the church lives.
Divine calling of the church	The church exists as a *witness* to God's mission, the *Missio Dei*. Getting in touch with this community is to be in touch with the very presence of God.
Church as human manifestation of God's mission	The church as a countercultural community seeks to embody the presence of God as its people live under the reign of Christ.

Table 20: How Does the Church Witness
to God's Mission in a Post-Christian Era?

Theme	Comments
The church is called to be an *otherworldly* community.	The church is the "womb" in which new Christians are conceived. The church is:
	Called: chosen by God Community: the household of God Otherworldly: ruled by the values of the kingdom
	In the womb of the church, non-Christians "gestate" toward new birth.
The church proclaims and enacts God's mission in worship.	Worship *remembers* God's saving deeds; worship *anticipates* the completion of God's rescue (salvation) at the end of history. Thus worship does the mission of God. It proclaims and enacts the salvation of the world.
The church nurtures its people into full maturity in Christ.	The church forms its people to put off evil, learn submissiveness, watch and pray, and resist the devil through an intentional process of formation.
A process for Christian formation.	Put off; submit; watch and pray; resist the devil

Questions for Discussion

1. Summarize your church's self-understanding.
   What does it mean for you to be church in this neighborhood? Are you a spiritual womb in which the newly conceived can grow?
2. Discuss each of the theological themes of the church and ask what these theological themes say to us.
   a. church and spirit
   b. the divine calling of the church
   c. the church as a human manifestation of God's mission
3. How does your congregation currently carry out the mission of God?
4. Discuss how the ancient church carried out the mission of God and how its approach may be of benefit to you.
   a. The church is called to be an *otherworldly* community.
   b. The church proclaims and enacts God's mission in worship.
   c. The church nurtures its people into full maturity in Christ through an intentional process of maturation.

CONCLUSION

My goal has been to respond to the challenge of the International Consultation on Discipleship and suggest a way into the future. In the final plenary session of the International Consultation a summary of planned actions was presented to the entire body. I will conclude this book by noting how the adaptation of the principles of ancient evangelism addresses the future concerns articulated by the International Consultation in their summary.

First, the summary confesses that there is a "need to break out of our conventional ways of presenting the word of God." It seems to be hard to break out of recent traditions from the nineteenth and twentieth centuries. Frequently leaders will reassert what has been effective in the recent past and dogmatically affirm that what is needed in the future is more commitment, more passion, and a renewed effort to restore the old ways. *Ancient-Future Evangelism* affirms an unchanging message in a changed world. It does not ask leaders to change the message but to acknowledge that we live in a post-Christian world in which previously successful models simply don't work anymore. The answer is not a fresh resurrection of recent methods but a determined effort to know how God's saving message can be communicated in a new cultural context. Careful reflection on today's culture shows that Christianity must stop reinventing itself in cultural accommodation and instead return to the countercultural vision of the faith embodied in a community of committed people. To do this we must "break out of our conventional ways" of doing ministry.

Second, the summary recognizes that future evangelism and Christian formation will take place in community. The summary calls on all Christians to begin Christian formation with "personal discipleship" at home in order to form "children" and "focus on character formation." Then formation needs to continue in the context of the church. We live in a society in which the sights and sounds of counter-Christian values continually bombard the individual consciousness, forming and altering lives toward values that are not Christian. The ancient process of Christian formation, born in a secular and pagan world, called for formation within the church. It understood the temptations and the allures of pagan influences and created communal ways of forming and transforming people into the image of Christlikeness. Congregations that adapt the ancient model must do so within community. If community does not exist in a local church, a commitment to become community must be made as the adaptation of the ancient process is being carried out.

Next, the International Consultation's summary acknowledges that "there is no quick fix. Discipleship takes commitment and it takes time—maybe a long time." The process of evangelism, discipleship, spiritual formation, and Christian vocation adapted from the early church is not easy. Leaders who are committed to provide leadership to this new model will need to take the time to carefully study it even as they do it. Groups will need to reflect on the ancient process, examine the suggested adaptation, and make changes that will allow the process and its context to be translated into their own indigenous culture. In the local church a core group of people may read and discuss and preferably walk through the process themselves before using the process to reach people outside the church. One pastor friend created a six-week process for his congregation. During this short period of time the volunteers passed through the four stages and the passage rites in a summary form. Now the congregation is reaching out to others empowered by their knowledge and experience of the process.

Finally, we return again to the reason for the International Consultation to meet in the first place—the great need to address "growth without depth," lives that are not characterized by "purity, integrity and holiness," and a "lack of power in the church to impact our cultures." Can this be changed? I think so, but not without a radical rethinking of how we carry new converts into a long obedience in the same direction.

In *Ancient-Future Evangelism* I have not offered something new or innovative. I simply have asked us to root evangelism and Christian formation in the biblical mandate of faith, then draw from a model that was established in a secular and pagan world of the first three centuries, and finally translate this model into an authentic process of initial Christian formation in our post-Christian world. Any local church in any part of the world can do this. In the third century this form of evangelism and Christian formation was practiced in every corner of the Roman Empire. No one has statistics on its effect, but the mention of it by nearly every prominent church writer of the third, fourth, and even fifth centuries suggests it was as widespread in that pagan culture as mass evangelism has been in the nineteenth and twentieth centuries. Considering our cultural shift into a post-Christian world, it seems reasonable to assert that this ancient approach to evangelism and Christian formation has the same potential to thrive today as it did then. The challenge of today and the future church is to become a faith-forming community, a place where people are not only born anew but formed into lifelong disciples of Jesus Christ.

APPENDIXES

APPENDIX 1

VARIOUS SEQUENCES FOR THE STAGES AND PASSAGE RITES

I have suggested that ancient-future evangelism can be adopted for a variety of different church traditions without sacrificing its unique structure of Christian formation. What is essential to the process of making initial disciples is the commitment to the four stages of conversion, discipleship, spiritual formation, and Christian vocation and to the passage rites that signify the transitions from one stage to the next.

These four stages and three passage rites will differ slightly in sequence depending on *when baptism occurs*—whether it takes place immediately after conversion or is delayed until the converting person has passed through the stages of discipleship and spiritual formation. Another issue that will determine the sequence of the stages and passage rites is the matter of *infant baptism*. How can churches that practice infant baptism adapt the model of ancient evangelism, which was based primarily on adult baptism? Finally, an alteration of the process must be made for people who wish to make a *reaffirmation of faith*. This sequence is for those who have been previously baptized either as infants or on a profession of faith, who fell away from the faith and the church, and who now want to return to the faith and inclusion in the church.

The models below illustrate how the four stages and three passage rites may be maintained in all four of these situations. Simply identify which sequence best represents your tradition, then follow it making adjustments and changes that best suit the way your church can most effectively become a faith-forming community.

Table 21: The Sequence for the Delay of Baptism

Stage	Goal	Passage Rite	Resource
Seeker	conversion	rite of conversion	*Follow Me!*
Hearer	discipleship	rite of covenant	*Be My Disciple!*
Kneeler	spiritual formation	rite of baptism	*Walk in the Spirit!*
Faithful	incorporation and vocation		*Find Your Gift!*

Table 22: The Sequence for Immediate Baptism

Stage	Goal	Passage Rite	Resource
Seeker	conversion	rite of baptism	*Follow Me!*
Hearer	discipleship	rite of covenant	*Be My Disciple!*
Kneeler	spiritual formation	rite of the reaffirmation of baptism	*Walk in the Spirit!*
Faithful	Christian vocation		*Find Your Gift!*

Table 23: The Sequence for Infant Baptism

Stage	Goal	Passage Rite	Resource
Infancy	inclusion in the church family	rite of infant baptism	
Hearer (sixth grade)	discipleship	rite of confirmation	*Follow Me!* *Be My Disciple!*
Kneeler (junior high)	spiritual formation	rite of reaffirmation of baptism	*Walk in the Spirit!*
Faithful (senior high)	Christian vocation		*Find Your Gift!*

Table 24: The Sequence for the Reaffirmation of Faith

Stage	Goal	Passage Rite	Resource
Lapsed Christian—one who has been baptized and is now returning to faith	rediscovery of faith	rite of welcome	*Follow Me!*
Hearer	discipleship	rite of covenant	*Be My Disciple!*
Kneeler	spiritual formation	rite of affirmation of baptism	*Walk in the Spirit!*
Faithful	Christian vocation		*Find Your Gift!*

The four stages are clearly presented in a video: *Journey to Jesus: The Worship, Evangelism, and Nurture Mission of the Church.* See www.ancientfutureworship.com.

Once you have identified the sequence your church will follow in its faith-forming process, the next step is to plan the passage rites you will use. Appendix 2 presents the basic content and use of the passage rites. Read and study the comments on the passage rite you will be using and develop rites suitable to your community.

APPENDIX 2

DESCRIPTIONS
OF THE PASSAGE RITES

Passage rites have the performative power to help a person mark the spiritual journey from one stage to another with "stones of remembrance." They provide the new Christian with public events that symbolize spiritual growth. When the whole congregation is appropriately involved in these public spiritual events, they become occasions for accountability, not only for the person passing through the rite but also for the entire congregation. This is because a passage rite includes (1) a renunciation of a former way of life, (2) a transition into a new way of life, and (3) a commitment of transformation.

Each passage rite has been listed below and briefly explained. Each congregation may choose a passage rite that relates to its own tradition and make changes to it that best reflect the style and purposes of the congregation.

1. The Rite of Conversion

The passage rite of conversion is used to publicly confirm that repentance, change of heart, and a new birth has occurred. This rite may be used as the first rite. It occurs anytime after a conscious conversion has been made. Or, if the congregation is following the Christian year as an organizing pattern for ancient-future evangelism, the rite will occur on the first Sunday of Advent. The converting persons are invited to come to the front of the church. If they are coming into the church through the witness of personal mentors, the mentors come with them and stand behind them. The mentors may lay hands on the shoulders of the converts.

The content of the rite of conversion may include brief questions and answers, which may be directed one-on-one or to the whole group at the same time. The questions and answers should include statements that clearly renounce Satan and all his works and affirm a turning to Jesus as Lord and Savior as well as words of commitment to be his disciple.

The symbols of conversion are equally important. They may include a cross and a Bible with an admonition about the significance of each. This ritual may also include a prayer for the sealing of the Holy Spirit, the sign of peace, and the directive to "take your seat among us as a sign of your belonging to the household of faith."

2. The Rite of Covenant

This passage rite comes after the time of initial discipleship and before the time of spiritual formation. It is a rite that signifies the end of initial discipleship and a transition to the stage of spiritual formation. The content of the rite of covenant points to the progress the new Christian has made in the stage of discipleship and to the commitment the new Christian now makes to initial spiritual formation that will result in baptism. In the ritual, affirmation should be made of the initial discipleship such as, "You have been on a journey. . . . During this journey you have studied. . . . You have deepened your spirituality by. . . . Now you are about to embark on a new phase of your initial journey into the faith." Next, the minister will ask questions that imply continued faith and the desire to go deeper into the faith and proceed toward baptism.

This stage is also accompanied by the powerful symbol of the rite of covenant—namely writing one's name in the book of covenant to express a deepening commitment to live the life of the disciple and proceed toward baptism. The converting persons are called up front where a table with an open book is in full view of the congregation. After the verbal commitment to go deeper into the faith and proceed toward baptism is made, the covenanting person, with his or her mentor, walks to the table. As the converting person signs the book of covenant, the mentor places his or her hands on the shoulders of the converting person. The two then may pass the kiss of peace. As they do, the congregation may sing the Celtic Alleluia or some other appropriate song or chorus.

This rite may occur at any time after a person has completed *Be My Disciple!* If the congregation is following the Christian year, this rite occurs on the first Sunday of Lent. They then enter the stage of the kneeler and study *Walk in the Spirit!* as they prepare for baptism.

3. The Rite of Baptism

Of all the rites of passage, the rite of baptism is the most crucial. It is the only one affirmed in the New Testament and used throughout the history of the church to bespeak an identity with the death and resurrection of Jesus. While all the other rites of passage referred to in this book are optional but useful, the rite of baptism is never presented as optional. It is the rite *par excellence* that identifies the person with his or her relationship with Jesus Christ. We are buried with him and are raised with him to newness of life as Paul indicates in Romans 6.

When should you baptize? Some churches will want to baptize immediately after conversion, whereas other congregations will choose the delay of baptism and put baptism at the end of the process of initial conversion. Some congregations will baptize adult converts only, whereas some congregations will baptize infants. I suggest that congregations follow the practice of their particular tradition. When the ancient model is followed, baptism will occur in the great paschal vigil (the Saturday night of Easter eve) or in the Easter sunrise service.

While the content of the baptismal service will follow the tradition of the local church, it should emphasize the historic elements of renunciation, of turning away from sin *(metanoia)*, and of turning to Jesus Christ as Lord and Savior.

There are many symbols that express this great transformation. Three primary symbols are the renunciation, the baptism itself, and the anointing with oil. The renunciation may include not only verbal words of renouncing Satan and all his ways of death but an actual spit in the face of the devil or a shaking off of the devil such as shaking one's foot before entering the water or of clenching a fist in the face of the evil one. This may be followed by baptism into the water using the words of the Apostles' Creed. The minister says, "Do you believe . . ." The one being baptized says, "I do," and is then baptized in the name of the Father, the Son, and the Holy Spirit. Then, as the person ascends out of the water, he or she may be anointed with oil to symbolize the reception of the Holy Spirit (Eph. 1:13) and finally be dressed in a white robe (Rev. 7:9) to festoon the baptized state.

4. The Rite of Welcome

The rite of welcome may also be used as a rite of initial relationship with Jesus Christ. This use is especially true for those congregations that feel that conversion is connected with the rite of baptism and that baptism should follow rather than precede the time of Christian formation.

In this case the rite of welcome is used after the seeker stage as a passage rite into the stage of discipleship. In this usage the rite of welcome acknowledges the seeker has gone beyond seeking to now explore more fully the commitment to discipleship. Conversion is seen as a continuing process that will culminate in baptism. En route the rite of welcome is primarily seen as a commitment to enter the final stage of preparation for baptism and the culminating passage rite of conversion.

In the ancient church the rite of welcome contained the content of an initial turning away from the powers of evil. Questions were asked such as, "Do you renounce all false worship?" and, "Do you turn to Jesus Christ?" The symbolism of the ancient church in the rite of welcome was also very strong. It included the sign of the cross and taking a seat among the faithful.

While all the content and symbolism of the rite of welcome does not go as far as the content and symbolism of baptism, it clearly indicates that an initial *metanoia* has taken place and that the spiritual journey toward full conversion is on its way. In the early church people admitted to the rite of welcome were considered Christians. They were told if they were martyred before their baptism, their blood would be their baptism.

Today congregations may use the rite of welcome as an expression of initial conversion, recognizing that the converted person is on the journey toward baptism and full participation in the life of the church.

5. The Rite of Confirmation

The rite of confirmation is used in those churches that practice infant baptism. It is used after confirmation class or after *Follow Me!* and *Be My Disciple!* Through the rite of confirmation the young believers confirm that they have embraced the meaning of their infant baptism and have entered into a personal discipleship relationship with Jesus Christ.

Congregations that practice confirmation may use their own rites, personalizing them to allow the confirmed to express personal commitment to continue to renounce Satan and all his works. This rite will also express the desire to enter the stage of spiritual formation.

The symbols used in this rite may draw from the rite of conversion and the rite of covenant. Use the gifts of the cross and the Bible, and call upon these young people to write their names in the book of covenant as they transit to the stage of spiritual formation. The rite of confirmation may occur at any time. For those churches following the Christian year, the rite will occur on the first Sunday of Lent, usually during the morning service. Mentors may place their hands on the shoulders of those to be confirmed during prayers on their behalf and/or during the writing of their names in the book of covenant.

6. The Rite for the Reaffirmation of Baptismal Vows

The rite for the reaffirmation of baptismal vows is used for those baptized as infants and for those who were previously baptized, became lapsed, and now are returning to faith and to the church. The rite for the reaffirmation of baptism may be used in place of baptism or may accompany baptism if there are two sets of people—new Christians being baptized for the first time and those baptized as infants who now affirm their baptismal vows or lapsed Christians who were baptized and are now returning to the faith.

The persons who are reaffirming their baptismal vows are called to the front. They stand with their mentors, who place their hands on their shoulders. Questions are asked pertaining to the reaffirmation of their original vows. Do they reaffirm their renunciation of evil, their faith in Christ, their willingness to be a disciple of Jesus? A prayer may be said thanking God for the uses of water as the water is poured into a bowl. This prayer will affirm that God created the world out of water, that water brought Noah and his family to safety, that Israel crossed over into the Promised Land through the waters of Jordan, that water signifies our relationship with Christ, that we are baptized into his death and resurrection. As the congregation sings a baptismal song, the water is sprinkled on the persons who reaffirm their faith (one may use an evergreen branch) and, as the people continue to sing, the water may be sprinkled over the entire congregation.

This service may close with a prayer and with the passing of the peace, especially to those who have just reaffirmed their faith.

The passage rites are presented in a video: *Journey to Jesus: The Worship, Evangelism and Nurture Mission of the Church*. See www.ancient futureworship.com.

APPENDIX 3

THE CHRISTIAN YEAR SEQUENCE

The ideal way to establish a faith-forming rhythm in the local church is to follow the pattern of the Christian year. For those churches that follow the Christian year, the sequence will be as follows.

Pentecost Sunday

On this day of the coming of the Holy Spirit, the church may commission those who feel called to evangelism. These people may commit to one-on-one relationships with unchurched friends and neighbors using *Follow Me!* as a connecting point for discussion. Or others may feel committed to establishing a neighborhood social and spiritual community. These people make a special effort in the season after Pentecost (summer and fall) to do effective evangelism.

First Sunday of Advent

New converts are presented to the church on the first Sunday of Advent using the rite of passage chosen by the church (rite of conversion, rite of baptism, rite of welcome). The mentor who led the new convert to Christ stands with the new believer through the rite of passage. The new convert now engages in discipleship using *Be My Disciple!* during the seasons of Advent, Christmas, and Epiphany in a continued one-on-one relationship or small group study.

Lent

On the first Sunday of Lent, the new disciple is carried through another rite of passage (rite of covenant, rite of confirmation). This passage rite signifies movement into the period of spiritual formation. During this period, which lasts for six weeks, the maturing Christian studies *Walk in the Spirit!* with his or her mentor or in a small group study.

Easter

Lent ends and Easter begins with the final passage rite (baptism, reaffirmation of baptism) on Easter Sunday. Now the new Christian enters into the final period of initial faith forming. During the Easter season (the seven weeks from Easter to Pentecost) the new Christian engages in the study of *Find Your Gift!* with his or her mentor or in a small group study.

Conclusion

Once this rhythm has been established, it has the power to affect the entire congregation in a meaningful way. The entire life of the congregation may be continuously formed in the pattern of evangelism, discipleship, spiritual formation, and Christian vocation. This rhythm can be extended to worship, to preaching, and to studies in faith formation that go beyond the initial training suggested in this book.

APPENDIX 4

THE EASTBOURNE CONSULTATION JOINT STATEMENT ON DISCIPLESHIP

International Consultation on Discipleship
September 24, 1999
Eastbourne, England

When our Lord Jesus was about to ascend into heaven, He commissioned His followers to go and make disciples of all nations, baptizing them, and teaching them to obey everything He had commanded them (Matt. 28:18–20). This comprises the mission given to His people today.

Given that this is our mission, it is of absolute and critical importance that we understand just what Jesus was commanding us to do. Jesus said "... anyone who does not carry his cross and follow me cannot be my disciple" (Luke 14:27). Thus, Jesus made it clear that true disciple-

This statement was drafted during and throughout the four days of the Eastbourne Consultation on Discipleship, September 21–24, 1999. During those brief days, the document was revised six times to address more than one hundred comments and recommendations from church leaders from over fifty-four countries and representing nearly ninety organizations, denominations, and churches. This final statement was presented as a final document at the concluding plenary session of the Consultation.

ship, at its very core, is a matter of the heart, and a matter of radical submission to His Lordship.

Acknowledgment of the Need

As we face the new millennium, we acknowledge that the state of the Church is marked by a paradox of growth without depth. Our zeal to go wider has not been matched by a commitment to go deeper. Researchers and pollsters have documented the fact that many times:

1. Christians are not that different from the culture around them. When the desert wind blows, it shapes the sand, and the Church has become more like the sand than the wind.
2. We grieve that many within the Church are not living lives of biblical purity, integrity and holiness. The need is in the pulpit and pew alike.
3. The lack of true discipleship has resulted in a lack of power in the Church to impact our culture.

Definition of Discipleship

While there are valid differences of perspective on what constitutes discipleship, we define Christian discipleship as a process that takes place within accountable relationships over a period of time for the purpose of bringing believers to spiritual maturity in Christ. Biblical examples suggest that discipleship is both relational and intentional, both a position and a process. We become disciples by turning from sin through repentance and turning to God through faith. The process of discipleship is played out in a vital life-giving relationship to God that enables us to walk in the light as He is in the light, and do the will of the Father (1 John 1:7; John 4:34). Jesus said if we hold to His teaching, then we are really His disciples (John 8:31), and we demonstrate this through loving one another (John 13:34–35).

The Marks of a Disciple

Although the process of identifying effective discipleship tools or methods is affected by the culture and setting, we affirm that

1. the life of a disciple is marked by submission to Christ. Jesus said that we cannot be His disciples unless we give up our very lives (Luke 14:27).
2. the marks of true repentance in the life of a disciple are evidenced by ongoing transformation, personal holiness, compassionate service, and the fruit of the Spirit (Galatians 5:22).

We acknowledge that perfection will not be achieved until we see Him face to face. True disciples do fail and are marked by humble repentance in response to personal failure, but recognize God's forgiveness and restoration in the journey.

Our Commitment

In recognition of the state of the Church and the biblical mandate to make disciples of all nations (Matt. 28:18–20), personally and corporately, we

1. call the Church and commit ourselves to preaching the Gospel and making disciples among all peoples in all nations.
2. will not water down the cost of discipleship in order to increase the number of converts. We acknowledge that part of making disciples is teaching people to obey everything that Jesus commanded.
3. acknowledge that a local church is the primary community within which discipleship should take place.
4. will pursue the process of discipleship just as purposefully as the proclamation of the Gospel. Evangelism and discipleship must be seen as integral.
5. will strive to submit ourselves to Christ as Lord in every area of our lives, recognizing that we are subjects in the Kingdom of God.
6. acknowledge that prayer and worship, study and teaching of the Bible, fellowship in the context of God's people, and personal accountability are necessary elements of spiritual growth. We recommit ourselves to exercising these disciplines as part of a life of discipleship.
7. affirm unreservedly the uniqueness of Christ as the one name under heaven whereby we must be saved, the only mediator between God and man (Acts 4:12; 1 Timothy 2:5–6; John 14:6), but we resist the temptation to define simplistic solutions that suggest that there is only one method of growing in Christian maturity.

8. recognize that different people and different cultures have different learning and communication styles. We must accommodate those styles in our efforts to make disciples, and address the unique needs of men, women, young people and children.

9. commit to follow the model of our Lord who lived His life with His disciples, and affirm the vital role of mentoring in the discipleship process.

10. call churches to rigorously assess their existing structures and processes to determine if they provide the most effective means of making disciples.

11. commit to beginning the discipleship process as early in life as possible, recognizing that large numbers of people come to faith as children and youth (2 Timothy 3:14–15).

12. acknowledge that discipleship resources, including Bibles, are not readily available to large numbers of God's people in some countries of the world. We commit to doing all we can to make these resources available to those who need them.

13. refocus on Christ and Christ-likeness as revealed in Scripture. He is the perfect pattern for our discipleship, and by living as His disciples we bear fruit and bring glory to the Father (John 15:8).

14. affirm the role of the Holy Spirit as our teacher, and the One by whom we are led into all truth (John 14:26; John 16:13). The Holy Spirit convicts, guides, and empowers us in the process of discipleship.

15. acknowledge the need for our faith in Christ to impact our societies: our families, our workplaces, our communities and our nations, thus becoming salt and light in a dark world (Matt. 5:13–16).

NOTES

Introduction to the Ancient-Future Faith Series

1. This series was begun following the positive response to *Ancient-Future Faith*. The series will develop themes from *Ancient-Future Faith* into fully developed books aimed at ministry in the postmodern world of the twenty-first century.

Introduction

1. International Consultation on Discipleship, *The Eastbourne Consultation Joint Statement on Discipleship* (Eastbourne, England, 24 September 1999).

2. David Neff, "Make Disciples, Not Just Converts," *Christianity Today*, 25 October 1999.

3. Ibid.

4. *Eastbourne Consultation.*

5. Ibid.

6. Neff, "Make Disciples."

7. *Eastbourne Consultation.*

Chapter 1: The Way New Christians Have Been Formed

1. Philip Carrington, *The Primitive Christian Catechesis* (Cambridge: Cambridge University Press, 1940), 31–44.

2. Ibid.

3. Marvin Wilson, *Our Father Abraham: Jewish Roots of the Christian Faith* (Grand Rapids: Eerdmans, 1989), 113.

4. Robert Martin-Achard, *An Approach to the Old Testament*, trans. J. C. G. Greig (Edinburgh: Oliver & Boyd, 1965), 46, in Wilson, *Our Father Abraham*, 150.

5. Joseph Soloveitchik, quoted in Wilson, *Our Father Abraham*, 153. Original quote is found in Paul R. Carlson, *O Christian! O Jew!* (Elgin, Ill.: David C. Cook, 1974), 142–43.

6. For a general discussion of the Great Commission, see David J. Bosch, *Transforming Mission: Paradigm Shifts in Theology of Mission* (Maryknoll, N.Y.: Orbis, 1994), especially chap. 2, "Matthew: Mission as Disciple-Making."

7. Bosch, *Transforming Mission*, 76.

8. Ibid., 66.

9. Ibid., 67.

10. Ibid., 69.

11. Ibid. See also Bosch, "Luke-Acts: Practicing Forgiveness and Solidarity with the Poor" and "Mission in Paul: Invitation to Join the Eschatological Community," chaps. 3–4 of *Transforming Mission*, 84–180.

12. Ibid. See in particular Alan Kreider, *The Change of Conversion and the Origin of Christendom* (Harrisburg, Pa.: Trinity, 1999).

13. Ibid., xv. I am deeply indebted to Alan Kreider for the terms *believing, belonging,* and *behaving.* I refer to them frequently throughout this book.

14. Ibid., 3.

15. See a more full account of Justin's conversion in Kreider, *Change of Conversion,* 2–4.

16. Justin Martyr, *The First Apology of Justin Martyr,* 61, in Cyril C. Richardson, *Early Christian Fathers* (Philadelphia: Westminster, 1943), 282.

17. Ibid.

18. Ibid, 287.

19. For the full text of *Apostolic Tradition,* see Gregory Dix and Henry Chadwick, eds., *The Treatise on the Apostolic Tradition of St. Hippolytus of Rome,* 2d rev. ed. (Ridgefield, Conn.: Morehouse, 1972). For a study and application of *Apostolic Tradition,* see Robert E. Webber, *Celebrating Our Faith* (San Francisco: Harper & Row, 1986).

20. The two best books that deal with the historical dissolution of the ancient pattern of disciple making are The Murphy Center for Liturgical Research, *Made, Not Born: New Perspectives on Christian Initiation and the Catechumenate* (Notre Dame: University of Notre Dame Press, 1976) and Maxwell E. Johnson, *The Rites of Christian Initiation: Their Evolution and Interpretation* (Collegeville, Minn.: Liturgical, 1999).

21. Kreider, *Change of Conversion,* 36.

22. For an understanding of the medieval sacramental system, see Johnson, "Christian Initiation in the Middle Ages," chap. 6 of *Rites of Christian Initiation,* 177–226.

23. Ibid., 230.

24. Ibid., 239.

25. Ibid.

26. Ibid., 236.

27. See Pierre Babin with Mercedes Iannone, *The New Era in Religious Communication,* trans. David Smith (Minneapolis: Fortress, 1991), 24–29.

28. Ibid., 27.

29. Ibid., 28.

30. See Daniel Leichty, ed., *Early Anabaptist Spirituality: Selected Writings* (New York: Paulist, 1994).

31. For the impact of the Enlightenment on Christian formation, see Johnson, *Rites of Christian Initiation.*

32. See Kenneth J. Collins and John H. Tyson, *Conversion in the Wesleyan Tradition* (Nashville: Abingdon, 2001).

33. Rick Warren, *The Purpose-Driven Church: Growth without Compromising Your Message and Mission* (Grand Rapids: Zondervan, 1995), 144.

34. The illustration is taken from *The Purpose-Driven® Church* by Rick Warren. Copyright © 1995 by Rick Warren. Used by permission of Zondervan.

Part 1: The Process of Christian Formation

1. For more detail on knowing in community through a particular language that represents a paradigm shift, see Brad J. Kallenberg, *Live to Tell: Evangelism for a Postmodern Age* (Grand Rapids: Brazos, 2002).

Chapter 2: Make Disciples

1. *Eastbourne Consultation.*

2. See Dallas Willard, *The Divine Conspiracy: Rediscovering Our Hidden Life in God* (San Francisco: HarperSanFrancisco, 1998). He writes, "It is almost universally conceded today that you can be a Christian without being a disciple," 26.

3. Michael J. Wilkins, *Following the Master: A Biblical Theology of Discipleship* (Grand Rapids: Zondervan, 1992), 40. Chapter 2, "Jesus and Disciples Today," is a discussion of the various uses of the word *disciple* among evangelicals.

4. *Eastbourne Consultation.*

5. See *Precatechumenate, Catechumenate, Purification and Enlightenment,* and *Mystagogia and Ministries,* vols. 1–4 of *Christian Initiation Reader* (New York: William H. Sadlier, 1984).

6. Dix and Chadwick, *Treatise on the Apostolic Tradition.*

7. See also Robert E. Webber, *Journey to Jesus: The Worship, Evangelism and Nurture Missions of the Church* (Nashville: Abingdon, 2001).

8. *Eastbourne Consultation.*

9. Jean Danie'Lou and Herbert Musurillo, eds., *From Glory to Glory: Texts from Gregory of Nyssa's Mystical Writings* (New York: Charles Scribners & Sons, 1961), 145.

10. Ibid., 213.

11. Saint Cyril of Jerusalem, *Protocatechesis* 1, trans. Paul Harbins (Westminster, 1963), 1. *Fathers of the Church*, v. 61, quoted in Jeff Astley, Leslie J. Francis, and Colin Crowder, *Theological Perspectives on Christian Formation: A Reader on Theology and Christian Education* (Grand Rapids: Eerdmans, 1996), 235.

12. Peter Roche de Coppens, *The Nature and Use of Ritual: The Great Christian Documents and Traditional Blue-Prints for Human and Spiritual Growth* (Washington, D.C.: University Press of America, 1979), 138.

13. Arnold van Gennep, *The Rites of Passage*, trans. Monika B. Vizodom and Gabrielle L. Caffe (Chicago: University of Chicago Press, 1960), 189–90, in Frank C. Senn, *Christian Liturgy: Catholic and Evangelical* (Minneapolis: Fortress, 1997), 9. Read chapter 1, "The Repertoire of Rites," for an excellent survey of the use and significance of Christian rites.

14. The full text of the *Didache* is found in Richardson, *The Early Church Fathers.*

15. *Eastbourne Consultation.*

16. For insights into moral and spiritual development, see James W. Fowler, *Stages of Faith: The Psychology of Human Development and the Quest for Meaning* (San Francisco: HarperSanFrancisco, 1981); and Jeff Astley, Leslie J. Francis, and Colin Crowder, *Theological Perspectives on Christian Formation* (Grand Rapids: Eerdmans, 1996).

Chapter 3: Evangelism

1. Peter L. Berger, ed., *The Desecularization of the World: Resurgent Religion and World Politics* (Grand Rapids: Eerdmans, 1999), 3.

2. Ibid., 4.

3. Antonia Tripolitis, *Religions of the Hellenistic Roman Age* (Grand Rapids: Eerdmans, 2002).

4. Ibid., 116.

5. Ibid.

6. Ibid., 116–17.

7. Amy Oden, "God's Household of Grace: Hospitality in the Early Church," in Kenneth Tanner and Christopher Hall, eds., *Ancient and Postmodern Christianity: Paleo-Orthodoxy*

in the 21ˢᵗ Century: Essays in Honor of Thomas C. Oden (Downers Grove, Ill.: InterVarsity, 2002), 39.

8. Ibid., 41.

9. Ibid., 47–48.

10. Rodney Stark, *The Rise of Christianity: How the Obscure, Marginal Jesus Movement Became the Dominant Religious Force in the Western World in a Few Centuries* (San Francisco: Harper, 1996), 20.

11. Ibid., 19.

12. Robin Lane Fox, quoted in ibid., 20.

13. Nathan Mitchell, *Eucharist as Sacrament of Initiation, Forum Essays 2* (Chicago: Liturgy Training Publications, 1994), 89–90, in Johnson, *Rites of Christian Initiation*, 3.

14. David Fitch, "Saving Souls Beyond Modernity: How Evangelism Can Save the Church and Make it Relevant Again" (unpublished manuscript, Church on the Vine, Long Grove, Ill.), 9.

15. Ibid., 5.

16. Ibid., 9.

17. Randy Frazee, *The Connecting Church: Beyond Small Groups to Authentic Community* (Grand Rapids: Zondervan, 2001). This book is a Willow Creek Association publication that illustrates how the seeker church is attempting to take into consideration the epistemological shift into the postmodern way of receiving and assimilating truth.

18. Ibid., 31.

19. Ibid., 56.

20. Wayne A. Meeks, *The First Urban Christians: The Social World of the Apostle Paul* (New Haven: Yale University Press, 1984), 78, in Frazee, *The Connecting Church*, 56.

21. Frazee, *The Connecting Church*, 62–64.

22. Ibid., 66.

23. See in particular the following publications: Edward J. Blakely and Mary Gail Snyder, *Fortress America: Gated Communities in the United States* (Washington, D.C.: Brookings Institute, 1999); Philip Langdon, *A Better Place to Live: Reshaping the American Suburb* (Amherst, Mass.: University of Massachusetts Press, 1994); and John L. Locke, *The De-Voicing of Society: Why We Don't Talk to Each Other Anymore* (New York: Simon & Schuster, 1998).

24. See Robert Wuthnow, *Sharing the Journey: Support Groups and America's New Quest for Community* (New York: Free Press, 1994), 276, in Frazee, *The Connecting Church*, 138.

25. Frazee, *The Connecting Church*, 138.

26. See http://www.sojourn.org.

27. Daniel Montgomery, personal conversation, winter 2002.

28. Frazee, *The Connecting Church*, 177.

29. Ibid. See especially chapter 14, "Implementing Common Possessions," 228–39.

30. See Roy M. Oswald and Speed B. Leas, *The Inviting Church: A Study in New Member Assimilation* (New York: Alban Institute, 1987), 28.

31. For the general effectiveness of seeker churches, see Thom S. Rainer, *Surprising Insights from the Unchurched and Proven Ways to Reach Them* (Grand Rapids: Zondervan, 2001).

32. See Oswald and Leas, *The Inviting Church*, 28. Rainer also affirms through his research that family and friends are the greatest influence in evangelism and church membership. See Rainer, *Surprising Insights from the Unchurched*, figure 1.9, 48.

33. David Fitch, "Evangelism at Life on the Vine" (unpublished paper, Church on the Vine, Long Grove, Ill., June 2002), 1.

34. Fitch, "Saving Souls Beyond Modernity," 9.

35. Ibid.

36. Pierre Babin with Mercedes Iannone, *The New Era of Religious Communication* (Minneapolis: Fortress, 1991), 96.

37. Fitch, "Saving Souls Beyond Modernity," 6.

38. Ibid., 7.

39. Ibid.

40. Ibid.

41. See Robert E. Webber, *Worship Old and New*, 2d ed. (Grand Rapids: Zondervan, 1994); Gilbert Ostdiek, *Catechesis for Liturgy* (Washington, D.C.: Pastoral, 1986); and Sally Morgenthaler, *Worship Evangelism* (Grand Rapids: Zondervan, 1996).

42. Karen Howe, "Worship as Evangelism," *Acts 29: Newsletter of the Episcopal Renewal Ministries* (February 1988): 8.

43. John Calvin, *Institutes of the Christian Religion* (Grand Rapids: Eerdmans, 1989), bk. 3, chap. 1, 1, 463. Book 3 is on the Holy Spirit. This classic work should be read by all as it points away from works of self-righteousness to the witness of the Holy Spirit as the means by which God's grace is applied and to the witness of the Spirit as a source of Christian confidence. See also David F. Wells, *God the Evangelist: How the Holy Spirit Works to Bring Men and Women to Faith*, 2d ed. (Carlisle, England: World Evangelical Fellowship, 1997).

44. Gustave Bardy, *La Conversion au Christianisme*, 1, in Michael Green, *Evangelism in the Early Church* (Grand Rapids: Eerdmans, 1970), 144.

45. Green, *Evangelism in the Early Church*, 144–47.

46. See John P. Newport, *The New Age Movement and the Biblical World View: Conflict and Dialogue* (Grand Rapids: Eerdmans, 1998).

47. Robert E. Webber, *Follow Me!* (Wheaton: IWS Resources, 2001). See www.ancient futureworship.com.

Chapter 4: Discipleship

1. Bill Hull, *The Disciple-Making Pastor: The Key to Building Healthy Christians in Today's Church* (Grand Rapids: Revell, 1988), 23.

2. Michael J. Wilkins, *Following the Master: A Biblical Theology of Discipleship* (Grand Rapids: Zondervan, 1992), 123.

3. Ibid., 132.

4. *Eastbourne Consultation*.

5. Cyprian of Carthage, *The Unity of the Catholic Church*, trans. Maurice Bevenot (Westminster, Md.: Newman, 1956; London: Longmans, Green and Co., 1957).

6. John Calvin, *Institutes of the Christian Religion*, trans. John Allen (Philadelphia: Presbyterian Board of Christian Education, 1813), bk. 4, ch. 2, 273.

7. Gregory S. Clapper, "From the 'Works of the Flesh' to the 'Fruit of the Spirit': Conversion and Spiritual Formation in the Wesleyan Tradition," in Kenneth J. Collins and John H. Tyson, *Conversion in the Wesleyan Tradition* (Nashville: Abingdon, 2001), 222.

8. See Babin with Iannone, *New Era in Religious Communication*, especially chap. 6, 146–67.

9. Burton Scott Easton, trans., *The Apostolic Tradition of Hippolytus* (Cambridge: Cambridge University Press, 1934; New York: Archon Books, 1962), 54–56.

10. See Robert E. Webber, *Worship Old and New*, rev. ed. (Grand Rapids: Zondervan, 1994).

11. Rudolph Otto, *The Idea of the Holy* (New York: Oxford University Press, 1923).

12. See Astley, Francis, and Crowder, *Theological Perspectives on Christian Formation*, 249.

13. Cyril of Jerusalem, quoted in Regis A. Duffy, O.F.M., *On Becoming a Catholic: The Challenge of Christian Initiation* (San Francisco: Harper, 1984), 61.

14. Rainer, *Surprising Insights from the Unchurched*, 21.

15. Easton, *Apostolic Tradition of Hippolytus*, 43.

16. William Harmless, *Augustine and the Catechumenate* (Collegeville, Minn.: Liturgical, 1995), 42.

17. Ibid., 56.

18. Ibid., 235.

19. Ibid.

20. Ibid., 156.

21. Ibid., 160–61.

22. Ibid., 165.

23. Peter Brown, *Augustine of Hippo: A Biography* (Berkeley: University of California Press, 1967), 251, in Harmless, *Augustine and the Catechumenate*, 168.

24. Harmless, *Augustine and the Catechumenate*, 168.

25. Ibid., 169.

26. See Graham Johnston, *Preaching to a Postmodern World* (Grand Rapids: Baker, 2001); Michael Quicke, "Applying God's Word in a Secular Culture," *Preaching* 17, no. 4 (January-February 2002): 7–15.

27. *Eastbourne Consultation*.

28. Harmless, *Augustine and the Catechumenate*, 210–11.

29. Ibid., 236.

30. Hans-Ruedi Weber, *The Book That Reads Me* (Geneva, Switzerland: WCC Publications, 1995).

31. Easton, *Apostolic Tradition of Hippolytus*, 41.

32. Robert Clinton, quoted in Henry A. Simon, *Mentoring* (St. Louis: Concordia, 2001), 13.

33. Ibid.

34. Easton, *Apostolic Tradition of Hippolytus*, 41.

35. D. Michael Henderson, *John Wesley's Class Meetings: A Model for Making Disciples* (Napanee, Ind.: Evangel Publishing House), 1997.

36. Ibid., 13.

37. Robert E. Webber, *Be My Disciple!* (Wheaton: IWS Resources, 2001).

Chapter 5: Spiritual Formation

1. *Eastbourne Consultation*.

2. George Gallup Jr. with Timothy Jones, *The Next American Spirituality: Finding God in the Twenty-First Century* (Colorado Springs: Victor Cook Communications, 2000), 14–15.

3. Ibid., 41.

4. John P. Newport, *The New Age Movement and the Biblical Worldview: Conflict and Dialogue* (Grand Rapids: Eerdmans, 1998), xi.

5. Gallup with Jones, *The Next American Spirituality*, 43.

6. Alister E. McGrath, *Christian Spirituality* (Malden, Mass.: Blackwell, 1999), 2.

7. For an introduction to how Paul's theology shapes his understanding of spirituality, see C. P. M. Jones, "The New Testament," in Cheslyn Jones, Geoffrey Wainwright, and Edward Yarnold, *The Study of Spirituality* (New York: Oxford University Press, 1986), especially pp. 75–83.

8. For a broad review of the early church literature on the Christian life, see Francis X. Murphy, *The Christian Way of Life* (Wilmington, Del.: Michael Glazier, 1968).

9. Ibid., 23.

10. Ibid., 46.

11. Ibid., 80–81.

12. Cyril of Jerusalem, Lecture III on baptism, *Catechetical Lectures,* in Cyril Richardson, *Cyril of Jerusalem and Nemesius of Emessa, Library of Christian Classics,* IV (Philadelphia: Westminster, 1955), 96.

13. Easton, *Apostolic Tradition of Hippolytus,* 44.

14. Ibid.

15. For an introduction to this service, see Robert E. Webber, ed., *The Services of the Christian Year,* vol. 6, of the *Complete Library of Christian Worship* (Peabody, Mass.: Hendrickson, 1995), ch. 7.

16. Easton, *Apostolic Tradition of Hippolytus,* 44–46.

17. See especially Craig Alan Satterlee, *Ambrose of Milan's Method of Mystagogical Preaching* (Collegeville, Minn.: Liturgical, 2002); Paul W. Harkins, *St. John Chrysostom: Baptismal Instruction* (New York: Paulist, 1963); Harmless, *Augustine and the Catechumenate;* and Craig Satterlee and Lester Ruth, *Creative Preaching on the Sacraments* (Nashville: Discipleship Resources, 2001).

18. A. G. Hebert, trans., *Christus Victor* (London: Macmillan, 1950), 53, in Ian Gillman, "Constantine the Great in the Light of the *Christus Victor* Concept," in *Conversion, Catechumenate, and Baptism in the Early Church,* ed. Ivert Ferguson (New York: Garland Publishing, 1993), 172.

19. Harkins, *St. John Chrysostom,* 16–17.

20. Ibid., 21.

21. Ibid., 71.

22. Ibid., 77.

23. Ibid., 74.

24. Satterlee and Ruth, *Creative Preaching on the Sacraments,* 18.

25. Ibid., 21.

26. Ibid., 20.

27. Easton, *Apostolic Tradition of Hippolytus,* 44.

28. Anne Field, *From Darkness to Light: How One Became a Christian in the Early Church* (Ben Lomand, Calif.: Conciliation, 1992), 83.

29. Harmless, *Augustine and the Catechumenate,* 287.

30. Ibid., 281.

31. Robert E. Webber, *Walk in the Spirit!* (Wheaton: IWS Resources, 2001).

Chapter 6: Christian Vocation

1. Easton, *Apostolic Tradition of Hippolytus,* 48.

2. Ibid., 49.

3. A. J. Conyers, "The Listening Heart: Vocation as the Basis of Human Community" (Baylor University, Waco, 2001, photocopy), 3.

4. Ibid., 8.

5. Ibid., 15.

6. Ibid., 9.

7. R. Paul Stevens, *Liberating the Laity: Equipping All the Saints for Ministry* (Vancouver: Regent College Publishing, 1993), 25.

8. Greg Ogden, *The New Reformation: Returning the Ministry to the People of God* (Grand Rapids: Zondervan, 1990), 97.

9. *Didache,* in Richardson, *Early Christian Fathers,* 172–74.

10. Augustine of Hippo, in Harmless, *Augustine and the Catechumenate,* 258.

11. Ibid.

12. Ibid.

13. John and Debbie Wright, "Live from the UK," *Cutting Edge* 5, no. 2 (Vineyard Christian Fellowship, Evanston, Ill., spring 2001): 10–13.

14. Ibid., 12.

15. Ibid., 12–13.

16. Ibid., 12.

17. Ibid., 13.

18. R. C. D. Jasper and G. J. Cuming, eds., *Prayers of the Eucharist: Early and Reformed*, 2d ed. (New York: Oxford University Press, 1980), 22–23.

19. George Gingnas, trans., *Egeria: A Diary of a Pilgrimage* (New York: Newman, 1970), 125.

20. Justin Martyr, *The First Apology of Justin Martyr*, 66.

21. Tertullian, in Enrico Mazza, *The Celebration of the Eucharist: The Origin of the Rite and the Development of Its Interpretation* (Collegeville, Minn.: Liturgical, 1999), 123.

22. Robert E. Webber, *Find Your Gift!* (Wheaton: IWS Resources, 2001).

23. This video can be obtained through the web site www.ancientfutureworship.com (Wheaton, 2002).

Chapter 7: The World We Evangelize

1. Jean-François Lyotard, *The Postmodern Condition: A Report on Knowledge*, trans. Geoff Bennington and Brian Massumi (Minneapolis: University of Minnesota Press, 1984).

2. ABC News, *Nightline*, 23 May 2002.

3. Augustine, *Confessions*, trans. R. S. Pine-Coffin (New York: Penguin Books, 1961), 1:1.

4. Larry W. Hurtado, *At the Origins of Christian Worship* (Grand Rapids: Eerdmans, 1999), 4.

5. Tertullian, *Defuga in Persecutione*, vol. 4 of *The Ante-Nicene Fathers* (Grand Rapids: Eerdmans, 1972), 116–25.

6. LaTonya Taylor, "The Church of Oprah Winfrey," *Christianity Today*, 1 April 2002, 43.

7. Toby Lester, "Oh, Gods!" *Atlantic Monthly* 289, no. 2 (February 2002): 37.

8. Marvin Olasky, "The Greatest Spin Ever Sold," *World* 17, no. 16 (27 April 2002): 10.

9. For a development of these three views, see Robert E. Webber, *The Church in the World* (Grand Rapids: Zondervan, 1986).

10. For an expanded study of the next generation leadership, see Robert E. Webber, *The Younger Evangelicals: Facing the Challenges of the New World* (Grand Rapids: Baker, 2002).

11. See Rodney Clapp, *A Peculiar People: The Church as Culture in a Post-Christian Society* (Downers Grove, Ill.: InterVarsity, 1996); and Stanley Hauerwas and William H. Willimon, *Resident Aliens: A Provocative Christian Assessment of Culture and Ministry for People Who Know Something is Wrong* (Nashville: Abingdon, 1989).

12. See Steven Connor, *Postmodern Culture: An Introduction to Theories of the Contemporary* (Oxford, England: Blackwell, 1996).

13. Lyotard, *The Postmodern Condition*, xxiv.

14. See Dallas Willard, *The Spirit of the Disciplines* (New York: Harper & Row, 1988).

15. John P. Newport, *The New Age Movement and the Biblical Worldview: Conflict and Dialogue* (Grand Rapids: Eerdmans, 1998).

16. See Stanley Hauerwas, *After Christendom: How the Church Is to Behave If Freedom, Justice and a Christian Nation Are Bad Ideas* (Nashville: Abingdon, 1991).

17. Stanley J. Grenz and John R. Franke, *Beyond Foundationalism: Shaping Theology in a Postmodern Context* (Louisville: Westminster John Knox, 2001).

18. Babin with Iannone, *New Era in Religious Communication*.

19. See Thomas L. Friedman, *The Lexus and the Olive Tree: Understanding Globalization* (New York: Anchor, 2000).

20. Christopher Flavin et al., *State of the World 2002* (New York: W. W. Norton & Co., 2002).

21. Walter Laqueur, *The New Terrorism: Fanaticism and the Arms of Mass Destruction* (New York: Oxford University Press, 1999).

22. David Lyon, *The Information Society: Issues and Illusions* (Cambridge, England: Polity, 1994).

23. See Andrew Careaga, *eMinistry: Connecting with the Net Generation* (Grand Rapids: Kregel, 2001).

Chapter 8: The Story We Tell

1. See Gregory A. Boyd, *God at War: The Bible and Spiritual Conflict* (Downers Grove, Ill.: InterVarsity, 1997).

2. See Andreas J. Kostenburger and Peter T. O'Brien, *Salvation to the Ends of the Earth: A Biblical Theology of Mission* (Downers Grove, Ill.: InterVarsity, 2001). These authors deal with the sacrificial aspect of Jesus' mission. It is curious, though, that they write an entire biblical theology of mission without any reference to the enormous amount of material in the Scripture about God's war with the powers of evil.

3. See Gregory A. Boyd, *Satan and the Problem of Evil: Constructing a Trinitarian Warfare Theodicy* (Downers Grove, Ill.: InterVarsity, 2001).

4. See also the work of Hendrikus Berkhof, *Christ and the Powers* (Scottsdale, Pa.: Herald, 1977).

5. To understand how the work of Christ calls the church to a life of community and service, see Eberhard Arnold, *Why We Live in Community* (Farmington, Pa.: Plough, 1995).

6. See Boyd, "Christus Victor," chap. 9 of *God at War,* for a thorough analysis of the scriptural basis of the work of Christ that overcomes the powers of evil.

7. Irenaeus, *Against Heresies*, bk. 4 in Richardson, *Early Church Fathers*.

8. Ibid.

9. Ibid.

10. For an excellent interpretation of God's salvation from creation to re-creation, see Georges Florovsky, *Creation and Redemption* (Belmont, Mass.: Nordland, 1976).

11. See the discussion on creation in John Meyendorff, *Byzantine Theology* (New York: Fordham University Press, 1974), 129–37.

12. Saint Gregory of Nazianzen, quoted in Georges Florovsky, *Creation and Redemption* (Belmont, Mass.: Nordland, 1976), 46.

13. John P. Newport, *The New Age Movement and the Biblical World View: Conflict and Dialogue* (Grand Rapids: Eerdmans, 1998), x.

14. For an example of a "rule of faith," see Tertullian, *Against Praxeas,* in William A. Jurgens, *The Faith of the Early Fathers,* vol. 1 (Collegeville, Minn.: Liturgical, 1979), 154.

15. Bryan P. Stone, *Compassionate Ministry: Theological Foundations* (Maryknoll, N.Y.: Orbis, 1996), 145.

16. Meyendorff, *Byzantine Theology*, 139.

17. Ibid., 140.

18. Justin Martyr, *The Second Apology*, in *Ante-Nicene Fathers* (ANF), vol. 1, ed. A. Roberts and J. Donaldson (Grand Rapids: Eerdmans, 1979), 190, in Boyd, *Satan and the Problem of Evil*, 39.

19. Ibid., 41. See n. 21 in Boyd. Quote from Irenaeus, *Against Heresies* 5.26.2 ANF 1: 555.

20. Ibid., 41; Tatian, *Address to the Greeks*, 7, ANF, 2:8.

21. Boyd, *Satan and the Problem of Evil*, 43.

22. Florovsky, *Creation and Redemption*, 84.

23. Ibid., 85.

24. Ibid.

25. Ibid., 86.

26. For a presentation of the unity between matter and spirit, see J. P. Moreland and Scot B. Rae, *Body & Soul: Human Nature and the Crisis in Ethics* (Downers Grove, Ill.: InterVarsity, 2000).

Chapter 9: The Church That Tells the Story

1. See Robert E. Webber, *The Moral Majority: Right or Wrong?* (Westchester, Ill.: Cornerstone, 1981).

2. There are many old and new books on the missional understanding of the church. For older books, I suggest Lesslie Newbigin, *Foolishness to the Greeks: The Gospel and Western Culture* (Grand Rapids: Eerdmans, 1986); and Bosch, *Transforming Mission*. For a newer introduction to the missional church, see George Hunsberger and Craig Van Gelder, *The Church Between Gospel and Culture: The Emerging Mission in North America* (Grand Rapids: Eerdmans, 1986).

3. See Miroslav Volf, *After Our Likeness: The Church as the Image of the Trinity* (Grand Rapids: Eerdmans, 1988).

4. John Graham, personal correspondence, summer 2002.

5. Darrell Harris, sermon, Institute for Worship Studies, Orange Park, Fla., June 2002.

6. From Cyprian, *The Unity of the Catholic Church*, trans. Maurice Beuenot (Westminster, Md.: Newman, 1956; London: Longmans, Green and Co., 1957).

7. See Robert E. Webber, *Worship Old & New*, 2d ed. (Grand Rapids: Zondervan, 1994).

8. See Frazee, *The Connecting Church*.

BIBLIOGRAPHY

Introduction

Webber, Robert E. *Be My Disciple!* Wheaton: Ancientfutureworship, 2002.

———. *Find Your Gift!* Wheaton: Ancientfutureworship, 2002.

———. *Follow Me!* Wheaton: Ancientfutureworship, 2002.

———. *Journey to Jesus: The Worship, Evangelism and Nurture Mission of the Church.* Nashville: Abingdon, 2001.

———. *Journey to Jesus: A Six Part Introduction to Worship Evangelism.* Wheaton: Ancientfutureworship, 2003. Videocassette.

———. *Walk in the Spirit!* Wheaton: Ancientfutureworship, 2002.

(These resources are available through www.ancientfutureworship.com.)

Chapter 1: The Way New Christians Have Been Formed

Bosch, David J. *Transforming Mission: Paradigm Shifts in the Theology of Mission.* Maryknoll, N.Y.: Orbis, 1991.

Collins, Kenneth J., and John H. Tyson. *Conversion in the Wesleyan Tradition.* Nashville: Abingdon, 2001.

Johnson, Maxwell E. *The Rites of Christian Formation: Their Evolution and Interpretation.* Collegeville, Minn.: Liturgical, 1999.

Kneider, Alan. *The Change of Conversion and the Origin of Christendom.* Harrisburg, Pa.: Trinity, 1999.

Liechty, Daniel, ed. *Early Anabaptist Spirituality: Selected Writings.* New York: Paulist, 1994.

Wilson, Marvin R. *Our Father Abraham: Jewish Roots of the Christian Faith.* Grand Rapids: Eerdmans, 1989.

Chapter 2: Make Disciples

Astley, Jeff, Leslie J. Francis, and Colin Crowder. *Theological Perspectives on Christian Formation: A Reader on Theology and Christian Education.* Grand Rapids: Eerdmans, 1996.

Bell, Catherine. *Ritual Theory, Ritual Practice.* New York: Oxford University Press, 1992.

Driver, Tom F. *The Magic of Ritual: Our Need for Liberating Rites that Transform Our Lives and Our Communities*. San Francisco: Harper, 1991.

Eliade, Mircea. *Rites and Symbols of Initiation: The Mystery of Birth and Rebirth*. New York: Harper, 1958.

Fowler, James W. *Stages of Faith: The Psychology of Human Development and the Quest for Meaning*. San Francisco: Harper, 1981.

Grimes, Ronald L. *Beginnings in Ritual Stories*. Washington, D.C.: University Press of America, 1982.

Rochede Coppens, Peter. *The Nature and Use of Ritual: The Great Christian Documents and Traditional Blue-Prints for Human and Spiritual Growth*. Washington, D.C.: University Press of America, 1979.

Shaughnessy, James D., ed. *The Roots of Ritual*. Grand Rapids: Eerdmans, 1973.

Turner, Victor. *The Ritual Process: Structure and Anti-Structure*. New York: Aldine De-Gruyer, 1969.

Chapter 3: Evangelism

Berger, Peter L., ed. *The Desecularization of the World: Resurgent Religion and World Politics*. Grand Rapids: Eerdmans, 1999.

Brueggemann, Walter. *Biblical Perspectives on Evangelism: Living in a Three Storied Universe*. Nashville: Abingdon, 1993.

Careaga, Andrew. *eMinistry: Connecting with the Net Generation*. Grand Rapids: Kregel, 2001.

Coalter, Milton Jr., and Virgil Cruz, eds. *How Shall We Witness? Faithful Evangelism in a Reformed Tradition*. Louisville: Westminster John Knox, 1985.

Frazee, Randy. *The Connecting Church: Beyond Small Groups to Authentic Community*. Grand Rapids: Zondervan, 2001.

Green, Michael. *Evangelism in the Early Church*. Grand Rapids: Eerdmans, 1970.

Hauerwas, Stanley. *With the Grain of the Universe: The Church's Witness and Natural Theology*. Grand Rapids: Brazos, 2001.

Hunter, George G., III. *How to Reach Secular People*. Nashville: Abingdon, 1992.

———. *To Spread the Power: Church Growth in the Wesleyan Spirit*. Nashville: Abingdon, 1987.

Kallenberg, Brad J. *Live to Tell: Evangelism for a Postmodern World*. Grand Rapids: Brazos, 2002.

Kerr, Hugh T., and John M. Mulder. *Famous Conversions: The Christian Experience*. Grand Rapids: Eerdmans, 1983.

Meeks, Wayne. *The First Urban Christians: The Social World of the Apostle Paul*. New Haven: Yale University Press, 1984.

Morgenthaler, Sally. *Worship Evangelism*. Grand Rapids: Zondervan, 1996.

Newbigin, Lesslie. *Foolishness to the Greeks: The Gospel and Western Culture*. Grand Rapids: Eerdmans, 1986.

Pippert, Rebecca Manley. *Out of the Saltshaker and into the World: Evangelism as a Way of Life*. Downers Grove, Ill.: InterVarsity, 1979.

Pohl, Christine. *Making Room: Recovering Hospitality as a Christian Tradition*. Grand Rapids: Eerdmans, 1999.

Posterski, Donald. *Reinventing Evangelism: New Strategies for Presenting Christ in Today's World*. Downers Grove, Ill.: InterVarsity, 1989.

Rainer, Thom S. *Surprising Insights from the Unchurched and Proven Ways to Reach Them*. Grand Rapids: Zondervan, 2001.

Richardson, Rick. *Evangelism Outside the Box: New Ways to Help People Experience the Good News*. Downers Grove, Ill.: InterVarsity, 2000.

Scifres, Mary J. *Searching for Seekers: Ministry with a New Generation of the Unchurched*. Nashville: Abingdon, 1998.

Stark, Rodney. *The Rise of Christianity: How the Obscure Marginal Jesus Movement Became the Dominant Religious Force in the Western World in a Few Centuries*. San Francisco: Harper, 1996.

Swanson, Roger K., and Shirley F. Clement. *The Faith Sharing Congregation*. Nashville: Discipleship Resources, 1999.

Tanner, Kenneth, and Christopher Hall, eds. *Ancient and Postmodern Christianity: Paleo-orthodoxy in the 21st Century. Essays in Honor of Thomas C. Oden*. Downers Grove, Ill.: InterVarsity, 2002.

Tripolitis, Antoniá. *Religions of the Hellenistic-Roman Age*. Grand Rapids: Eerdmans, 2002.

Wuthnow, Robert. *Sharing the Journey: Support Groups and America's New Quest for Community*. New York: Free, 1994.

Chapter 4: Discipleship

Anderson, Ray S. *The Shape of Practical Theology: Empowering Ministry with Theological Praxis*. Downers Grove, Ill.: InterVarsity, 2001.

Arnold, Eberhard. *Why We Live in Community: With Two Interpretive Talks by Thomas Merton*. Farmington, Pa.: Plough, 1995.

Arnold, Jeffrey. *Starting Small Groups: Building Communities that Matter*. Nashville: Abingdon, 1997.

Astley, Jeff, Leslie J. Francis, and Colin Crowder. *Theological Perspectives on Christian Formation: A Reader on Theology and Christian Education*. Grand Rapids: Eerdmans, 1996.

Barry, William A., and William J. Connolly. *The Practice of Spiritual Direction*. San Francisco: Harper, n.d.

Batson, David. *The Treasure Chest of the Early Christians: Faith, Care and Community from the Apostolic Age to Constantine the Great*. Grand Rapids: Eerdmans, 2001.

Benedict, Daniel T. *Come to the Waters: Baptism and Our Ministry of Welcoming Seekers and Making Disciples*. Nashville: Discipleship Resources, 1996.

Bonhoeffer, Dietrich. *The Cost of Discipleship*. New York: Simon and Schuster, 1995.

Bushnell, Horace. *Christian Nurture*. Cleveland: Pilgrim, 1994.

Charry, Ellen T. *By the Renewing of Your Minds: The Pastoral Function of Christian Doctrine*. New York: Oxford University Press, 1997.

Fowler, James W. *Becoming Adult, Becoming Christian: Adult Development and the Christian Faith*. San Francisco: Jossey-Bass, 2000.

Groome, Thomas H. *Christian Religious Education: Sharing Our Story and Vision*. San Francisco: Jossey-Bass, 1980.

———. *Sharing Faith: A Comprehensive Approach to Religious Education and Pastoral Ministry*. Eugene, Ore.: Wipf and Stock, 1998.

Hall, Christopher. *Reading Scripture with the Church Fathers*. Downers Grove, Ill.: InterVarsity, 1998.

Harmless, William. *Augustine and the Catechumenate*. Collegeville, Minn.: Liturgical, 1995.

Henderson, Michael D. *John Wesley's Class Meeting: A Model for Making Disciples*. Nappanee, Ind.: Evangel, 1997.

Henricksen, Walter A. *Disciples Are Made Not Born*. Colorado Springs: Chariot Victor, 1988.

Horne, Herman. *Jesus the Teacher: Examining His Expertise in Education*. Grand Rapids: Kregel, 1998.

Houston, James M. *The Mentored Life: From Individualism to Personhood*. Colorado Springs: NavPress, 2002.

Hull, Bill. *The Disciple-Making Pastor: The Key to Building Healthy Christians in Today's Church*. Grand Rapids: Revell, 2001.

Nemeck, Francis Kelly. *The Way of Spiritual Direction*. Collegeville, Minn.: Liturgical, 1985.

Ogden, Greg. *Discipleship Essentials: A Guide to Building Your Life in Christ*. Downers Grove, Ill.: InterVarsity, 1998.

Old, Hughes Oliphant. *The Reading and Preaching of the Scriptures in the Worship of the Christian Church*. Vol. 2, *The Patristic Age*. Grand Rapids: Eerdmans, 1998.

Rotelle, John E., ed. *Augustine, Teaching Christianity: De Doctrina Christiana*. New York: New City, 1996.

Ruth, Lester. *Accompanying the Journey: A Handbook for Sponsors*. Nashville: Discipleship Resources, 1997.

Simon, Henry A. *Mentoring*. St. Louis: Concordia, 2001.

Watson, David Lowes. *Covenant Discipleship: Christian Formation Through Mutual Accountability*. Nashville: Discipleship Resources, 1998.

Weber, Hans-Ruedi. *The Book That Reads Me: A Handbook for Bible Study Enablers*. Geneva: WCC Publications, 1995.

Wilhoit, James C., and John M. Dettoni. *Nurture That is Christian: Developmental Perspectives on Christian Education*. Grand Rapids: Baker, 1995.

Wilkins, Michael J. *Following the Master: A Biblical Theology of Discipleship*. Grand Rapids: Zondervan, 1992.

Willard, Dallas. *The Divine Conspiracy: Rediscovering Our Hidden Life in God*. San Francisco: HarperSanFrancisco, 1998.

Chapter 5: Spiritual Formation

Arnold, Clinton E. *Powers of Darkness: Principalities and Powers in Paul's Letters*. Downers Grove, Ill.: InterVarsity, 1992.

Aulén, Gustav. *Christus Victor: An Historical Study of the Three Main Types of the Idea of the Atonement*. New York: Collier, 1969.

Balthasar, Hans Urs Von. *Prayer*. San Francisco: Ignatius, 1986.

Boyd, Gregory A. *Satan and the Problem of Evil: Constructing a Trinitarian Warfare Theodicy*. Downers Grove, Ill.: InterVarsity, 2001.

Callen, Barry. *Authentic Spirituality: Moving Beyond Mere Religion*. Grand Rapids: Baker Academic, 2001.

Collins, Kenneth J., ed. *Exploring Christian Spirituality*. Grand Rapids: Baker Academic, 2000.

Ferguson, Everett, David M. Scholar, and Paul Corby Finney. *Studies in Early Christianity*. Vol. 11, *Conversion, Catechumenate, and Baptism in the Early Church*. New York: Garland, 1993.

Finn, Thomas M. *Early Christian Baptism and the Catechumenate: Italy, North Africa, and Egypt*. Collegeville, Minn.: Liturgical, 1992.

Gallup, George, Jr. with Timothy Jones. *The Next American Spirituality: Finding God in the Twenty First Century*. Colorado Springs: Victor Cook, 2000.

Gingras, George, E., ed. *Egeria: Diary of a Pilgrimage*. New York: Newman, 1970.

Harkins, Paul W. *St. John Chrysostom: Baptismal Instructions*. New York: Paulist, 1963.

Harmless, William. *Augustine and the Catechumenate*. Collegeville, Minn.: Liturgical, 1995.

Jones, Cheslyn, Geoffrey Wainwright, and Edward Yarnold, eds. *The Study of Spirituality*. New York: Oxford University Press, 1986.

Kadloubovsky, E., and G. E. H. Palmer, trans. *Unseen Warfare: The Spiritual Combat and Path to Paradise of Lorenzo Scaupoli. Edited by Nicodemus of the Holy Mountain and revised by Theophan the Recluse*. Crestwood, N.J.: St. Vladimir Seminary Press, 1995.

Kenneson, Philip D. *Life on the Vine: Cultivating the Fruit of the Spirit in Christian Community*. Downers Grove, Ill.: InterVarsity, 1999.

McGrath, Alister. *Christian Spirituality*. Malden, Mass.: Blackwell, 1999.

Meyendorff, John. *St. Gregory Palamas and Orthodox Spirituality*. Crestwood, N.J.: St. Vladimir Seminary Press, 1974.

Murphey, Ed. *The Handbook for Spiritual Warfare*. Nashville: Thomas Nelson, 1992, 1996.

Murphy, Francis X. *The Christian Way of Life*. Wilmington, Del.: Michael Glazier, 1986.

Powell, Samuel M., and Michael E. Lodahl. *Embodied Holiness: Toward a Corporate Theology of Spiritual Growth*. Downers Grove, Ill.: InterVarsity, 1999.

Satterlee, Craig. *Ambrose of Milan's Method of Mystagogical Preaching*. Collegeville, Minn.: Liturgical, 2002.

Satterlee, Craig, and Lester Ruth. *Creative Preaching on the Sacraments*. Nashville: Discipleship Resources, 2001.

Schultze, Quentin J. *Habits of the High-Tech Heart: Living Virtuously in the Information Age*. Grand Rapids: Baker Academic, 2002.

Telfer, William. *Cyril of Jerusalem and Nemesius of Emessa*. Philadelphia: Westminster, 1955.

Turner, Paul. *The Hallelujah Highway: A History of the Catechumenate*. Chicago: Liturgical Training, 2000.

Wells, David R. *Losing Our Virtue: Why the Church Must Recover Its Moral Vision*. Grand Rapids, Eerdmans, 1998.

Willard, Dallas. *The Spirit of the Disciplines: Understanding How God Changes Lives*. San Francisco: Harper, 1991.

Willimon, William. *Remember Who You Are: Baptism, A Model for Christian Life*. Nashville: The Upper Room, 1980.

Willimon, William H., and Stanley Hauerwas. *Lord, Teach Us: The Lord's Prayer and the Christian Life*. Nashville: Abingdon, 1996.

Yarnold, Edward, S. J. *The Awe Inspiring Rites of Imitation: Baptismal Homilies of the Fourth Century*. Middlegreen, Slough, England: St. Paul, 1971.

Chapter 6: Christian Vocation

Christensen, Michael J., ed., with Carl E. Savage. *Equipping the Saints: Mobilizing Laity for Ministry*. Nashville: Abingdon, 2000.

Conyers, A. J. *The Listening Heart: Vocation as the Basis of Human Communities*. Baylor University, Waco, 2001, photocopy.

Ogden, Greg. *The New Reformation: Returning the Ministry to the People of God*. Grand Rapids: Zondervan, 1990.

Chapter 7: The World We Evangelize

Flavin, Christopher, et al. *State of the World 2002. A Worldwatch Institute Report on Progress Toward a Sustainable Society*. New York: W. W. Norton & Co., 2002.

Henderson, David W. *Culture Shift: Communicating God's Truth to Our Changing World*. Grand Rapids: Baker, 1998.

Jenkins, Philip. *The Next Christendom: The Coming of Global Christianity*. London: Oxford University Press, 2002.

Lyon, David. *The Information Society: Issues and Illusions*. Cambridge, England: Polity, 1994.

Snyder, Howard. *Earth Currents: The Struggle for the World's Soul*. Nashville: Abingdon, 1995.

Chapter 8: The Story We Tell

Abraham, William J. *The Logic of Evangelism*. Grand Rapids: Eerdmans, 1989.

Aulén, Gustaf. *Christus Victor: An Historical Study of the Three Main Types of the Idea of the Atonement*. New York: Collier, 1969.

Boyd, Gregory A. *God at War: The Bible and Spiritual Conflict*. Downers Grove, Ill.: InterVarsity, 1997.

———. *Satan and the Problem of Evil: Constructing a Trinitarian Warfare Theodicy*. Downers Grove, Ill.: InterVarsity, 2001.

Florovsky, Georges. *Creation and Redemption*. Belmont, Mass.: Nordland, 1976.

Kostenberger, Andreas J., and Peter T. O'Brien. *Salvation to the Ends of the Earth: A Biblical Theology of Mission*. Downers Grove, Ill.: InterVarsity, 2001.

Moreland, J. P., and Scott B. Rae. *Body and Soul: Human Nature and the Crisis in Ethics*. Downers Grove, Ill.: InterVarsity, 2000.

Russell, Jeffrey Burton. *The Price of Darkness: Radical Evil and the Power of God in History*. Ithaca, N.Y.: Cornell University Press, 1988.

Stone, Bryan P. *Compassionate Ministry: Theological Foundations*. Maryknoll, N.Y.: Orbis, 1996.

Chapter 9: The Church That Tells the Story

Bosch, David J. *Transforming Mission: Paradigm Shifts in Theology of Mission*. Maryknoll, N.Y.: Orbis, 1991.

Cardoza-Orlendi, Carlos F. *Mission: An Essential Guide*. Nashville: Abingdon, 2002.

Clapp, Rodney. *A Peculiar People: The Church as Culture in a Post-Christian Society*. Downers Grove, Ill.: InterVarsity, 1996.

Dawn, Marva. *Truly the Community: Romans 12 and How to Be the Church*. Grand Rapids: Eerdmans, 1992.

Foust, Thomas F., and others. *A Scandalous Prophet: The Way of Mission After Newbigin*. Grand Rapids: Eerdmans, 2002.

Gibbs, Eddie. *ChurchNext: Quantum Changes in How We Do Ministry*. Downers Grove, Ill.: InterVarsity, 2000.

Gruder, Darrell L., ed. *Missional Church: A Vision for the Sending of the Church in North America*. Grand Rapids: Eerdmans, 1998.

Hauerwas, Stanley, and William H. Willimon. *Resident Aliens: A Proactive Christian Assessment of Culture and Ministry for People Who Know That Something Is Wrong*. Nashville: Abingdon, 1989.

Hunsberger, George R., and Craig Van Gelder, eds. *The Church Between Gospel and Culture: The Emerging Mission in North America*. Grand Rapids: Eerdmans, 1996.

Hütter, Reinhard. *Suffering Divine Things: Theology as Church Practice*. Grand Rapids: Eerdmans, 1997.

Kirk, Andrew J., and Kevin J. Vanhoozer, eds. *To Stake a Claim: Mission and the Western Crisis of Knowledge*. Maryknoll, N.Y.: Orbis, 1999.

Schattauer, Thomas H., ed. *Inside Out: Worship in an Age of Mission*. Minneapolis: Fortress, 1999.

Vanderven, Johannes A. *Ecclesiology in Context*. Grand Rapids: Eerdmans, 1993.

Van Gelder, Craig. *The Essence of the Church: A Community Created by the Spirit*. Grand Rapids: Baker, 2000.

———, ed. *Confident Witness–Changing World: Rediscovering the Gospel in North America*. Grand Rapids: Eerdmans, 1999.

Volf, Miroslav. *After Our Likeness: The Church as the Image of the Trinity*. Grand Rapids: Eerdmans, 1998.

INDEX

Robert E. Webber is Myers Professor of Ministry at Northern Seminary, president of the Institute for Worship Studies, and emeritus professor of theology at Wheaton College. He is the author of more than forty books, including *Ancient-Future Faith* and *The Younger Evangelicals*, both published by Baker Books.

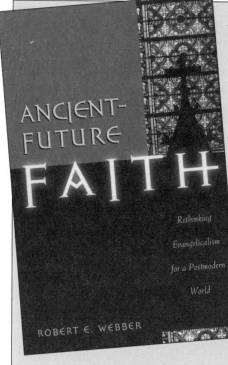

ANCIENT-FUTURE FAITH
Rethinking Evangelicalism for a Postmodern World

IN THIS PROVOCATIVE WORK, Robert E. Webber contends that present-day evangelicalism is a product of modernity. The way forward for evangelicalism begins with looking at the resources the early church tradition provides for making faith relevant in a postmodern world.

"This book makes an important contribution ... as a call for theological renewal within evangelical churches ... timely, practical, and persuasive."

—*Publishers Weekly*

"[A] well written and readable scholarly work with some interesting insights into this important segment of religion in America."

—*Library Journal*

"*The Agenda for Theology*, which I attempted to set forth in 1979, is here being significantly extended by Robert Webber ... in a way that is profoundly gratifying."

— **Thomas C. Oden,** professor of theology and ethics, Drew University

"Here is a faith for our time that finds in the ancient traditions the power to speak to the postmodern world. This book amounts to an introduction to Christianity from the theme of *Christus Victor*. It draws from Webber's own experience of growth as a hearer of God's Word and is backed up with an impressive set of endnotes, charts, and a bibliography."

— **Clark H. Pinnock,** professor of theology, McMaster Divinity College

"Robert Webber substantiates the vision of an anciently rooted and forward-looking evangelicalism that marks all of his work. *Ancient-Future Faith* works as a narrative-oriented Christian primer and as a road map to the promise of catholic evangelicalism. . . . Webber shows what it means to take seriously the character of Christian testimony as Christ-following church-formed story."

— **Gary Dorrien,** author, *The Remaking of Evangelical Theology*

"Now, more than ever, with the culture wars of a dying modernity cutting deeper and more darkly into desperation and anger, all evangelicalism needs to hear Bob Webber. Take up, read, pray, and consider: in this direction lies the most hopeful future of our faith."

— **Rodney Clapp,** author, *A Peculiar People*

THE YOUNGER EVANGELICALS
Facing the Challenges of the New World

A NEW EVANGELICAL AWAKENING is taking place around the world. And the changes are being introduced by an emerging generation of leaders— *The Younger Evangelicals.* Who are they and what is different about their way of thinking and practicing church? How are they keeping ministry up to speed with our rapidly changing culture? In this provocative and energizing book, they will tell you.

"If you're suspicious about new winds blowing across the evangelical coastland, please don't criticize until you've read The Younger Evangelicals. It is by far the most thoughtful description of what's going on. If you're not critical but just curious, Webber will give you a thorough immersion into the emerging church. And if you're 'younger' yourself or young at heart, you'll find Webber giving voice to much that you have felt but couldn't yet articulate. Webber proves himself a sagely resource for this fresh, fledgling movement in this wise, warm, timely book."

—**Brian McLaren,** pastor, author, senior fellow with Emergent (www.emergentvillage.com)

"At a time when many graying prognosticators are bemoaning the state of the church, it is refreshing to read a commentator of Robert Webber's stature who is optimistic about the future of the evangelical cause. Webber documents the presence of a cadre whom the Holy Spirit is raising up to lead the church in offering a biblically rooted, historically informed, and culturally aware gospel witness. I am personally encouraged by Webber's findings."

—**Stanley J. Grenz,** Distinguished Professor of Theology, Baylor University

"An eye-popping, brain-bending look at where the evangelical church must head if it has any hopes of impacting postmodern culture. A superbly researched, foundational work, it is easily the best primer on the emerging church that I have seen."

—**Sally Morgenthaler,** founder of Sacramentis.com, author of *Worship Evangelism*